DYSLEXIA:
Different Not Disabled

by Fred Thornhill

*A Dyslexic's Journey from ABC
to a Master's Degree*

Copyright © 2012 Fred Thornhill
All Rights Reserved.

ISBN-10: 1467957259
ISBN-13: 9781467957250

Library of Congress Control Number: 2011961539
CreateSpace, North Charleston, SC

Dedicated to my mother
whose unflagging faith and support enabled my success
in spite of unknowable odds

CONTENTS

Foreword i
Preface iii
Acknowledgements v

1. The Invitation 1
2. The Beginning. 5
3. Balmain C. M. School 11
4. San Fernando E. C. School 37
5. Naparima College. 59
6. The World of Work. 79
7. Sir George Williams University 89
8. Ryerson Polytechnical Institute 93
9. The Master's Programme 97
10. Drum, Trumpet, Flute, Apple, Saxophone. 105

Appendices:
   1. Simulation Group Exercise. 119
   2. Glossary 121
   3. Misspellings 123

FOREWORD

As a dyslexic person with dyslexic nieces and great nieces; as an educator, especially one who has devoted most of my teaching years to working with children with hidden disabilities; and as an educator seeking to be the best educator and advocate for children and young adults, I am delighted that Fred has written this book.

Dyslexia: Different not Disabled, is a book for parents, extended family members, teachers and young people who need extra support in and out of school to ensure their all-round healthy development. This book describes Fred's journey as a dyslexic from early childhood all the way through formal education, graduate school and a Master's Degree. What is particularly important is how the writer describes the social challenges he encountered, alerting his readers to the need for direct intervention in a dyslexic's life to ensure all aspects of their development.

Take time when reading this book. It is descriptive, yet not filled with jargon. The book is insightful and allows the reader to meet the main character and recognize his twin in their daily encounters. There are many lessons to be learnt. There are many ideas and strategies presented in this book that can be incorporated into the lives of children and young people with dyslexia. Fathers, grandparents and family members will better understand the child they feel "Mom is spoiling," "the lazy one," or "the trouble maker." They will be able to reconnect with their family member and build healthier relationships. Mothers will stop condemning themselves and become better copartners in supporting and mentoring their offspring. Teachers will begin to understand that Dyslexia does not mean an inability to "learn," or "stupid" and that the child's single goal is not to disrupt the class and disturb the teacher's carefully planned lesson. The village will respond more positively to the dyslexic person, and the phrase "you are really stupid," will be diminished.
This book will be of help to the Dyslexic communities. The techniques housed within this book will enhance the damaged self-esteem many dyslexic individuals encounter and help them to recognize their strengths. It will allow many to

succeed in spite of their condition, and reduce the waste of human capital lost because of the failure to understand their needs.

Remember, change will not happen overnight so celebrate every small success.

Enjoy reading the book. Use the lessons and apply the strategies. As a dyslexic person, I can testify that the road travelled was painful and rough. Let us work and ensure the all-round development of all children and young people who are challenged in any way. Let us create a different environment that would allow dyslexic children to unlock and open their gifts, even if they open them later.

Dr. Esla Lynch
Eshe's Learning Center

PREFACE

During the time that I was associated with the Faculty of Education at York University, Toronto, I was given the opportunity to share with in-service Special Education Teachers pursuing postgraduate certification my personal experiences from living with dyslexia. Recently, a friend who was a Special Education Professional to have been in the class where I first told my story, said that the information I shared gave her a better understanding of dyslexia and helped her in her professional career. She challenged and encouraged me to document my experience. I decided to accept the challenge in the hope that it might benefit others.

In Appendix 1, I have included a simulation exercise designed to allow non-dyslexic individuals to gain a better understanding of some of the problems dyslexic children encounter in the classroom

To assist the reader I have created as Appendix 2, a glossary of the words and phrases that need explanation, all the colloquialisms and slang words unique to the Trinidad and Tobago culture that appear in the text and I have used superscripts to identify them.

Shortly after I began working on the manuscript, I became aware of the number of spelling mistakes I was making. In some instances, I was reversing letters, while in other instances I was simply misspelling the words. Even I was surprised at how many of these spelling mistakes I still make. Although I did not capture them all, as AutoCorrect made many corrections before I had a chance to intervene, I thought that including the *misspelling*s might be helpful in providing the reader with additional insights into my world. Therefore, I have corrected and italicized the words that I had misspelled and I have included the correctly spelt words along with the original misspellings in Appendix 3.

ACKNOWLEDGEMENTS[1]

I wish to express my gratitude to the people who have made valuable contributions to the creation of this work.

There are those special people gifted with the ability to ask a simple question and provide guidance, helping individuals to realize their potential. One such person is Imogen Foster-Algoo. She was the person who planted the seed that led to the creation of this work. In a casual conversation about my writing, she mentioned that she was in the class when Dr. Bowers first invited me to tell my Dyslexia story. Imogen asked a simple question, "Why don't you share it?" I understood what she meant. Imogen and her husband, Stanley, formed a support team that read my drafts and asked pertinent questions that awakened memories hidden in the deep recesses of my mind, but which needed telling to complete the story. I graciously acknowledge the contribution made by Imogen and Stanley Algoo.

I would also like to acknowledge Miss Eldica Baxter, who ensured that I received a solid educational foundation, without which I never would have been able to write; Miss Sybil James, whose concern about my predicament moved her to seek a cure for my condition; Miss Beulah Meghu for her patience and understanding as she catered to my educational needs; Dr. Joan Bowers, Faculty of Education, York University, Toronto, who first convinced me that my story could be helpful to others and invited me to share it with her class of in-service teachers; Janet Baptiste-John for getting me involved in her workshops; Dr. Esla Lynch, who invited me to participate in her seminars and made it possible for me to share my story with concerned parents and dedicated teachers, and who also read my manuscript and wrote the foreword; and Maureen Henry, my editor.

---

1 Miss Eldica Baxter subsequently lectured at the Government Teachers' Training College: Miss Beulah Meghu became Principal of Naparima Girls' High School and Jit Ganessingh was honoured by Her Majesty the Queen for his poetry.

CHAPTER 1

THE INVITATION

Dr. Joan Bowers had completed her introductions, so here I stood in Curtis Lecture Hall L at York University, Toronto looking into the faces of five hundred in-service teachers. They had enrolled in a Special Education programme and were anxiously waiting to hear how I, a recent immigrant who had grown up in a rural village in Trinidad, had successfully obtained my Master's Degree despite my peculiar way of looking at the world. Although in current educational jargon I would be labelled 'dyslexic,' I had no specific intervention to assist me on my educational journey.

The events of the previous few weeks had conspired to bring me to this juncture. The first involved Dr. Daphne Shiff, a very progressive Natural Science professor at the university. Dr. Shiff was one of the professors who was willing to spend the time necessary to provide her students with a richer learning experience through the innovative use of television. The Television Centre provided the production facilities while the Natural Science Department was responsible for the content. The departments shared the cost of production.

It was my responsibility to tabulate the cost of each experiment. The Natural Science Department's share of the cost of producing the latest televised experiments amounted to one thousand six hundred and fifty-four dollars ($1,654).

I met with Dr. Shift to review the project, determine how we could improve the production element of her future productions and to present her with the charges associated with her latest production. I read the final figure, "One thousand, five hundred sixty-four," before placing the neatly typed statement on the desk in front of her.

"What did you say?" she asked as she looked at the statement and reached for her pen. Normally I would have become unsure of myself and assumed that I had read the numbers wrong, but when I saw her casually reaching for her pen, I dismissed it thinking that she just wanted to make some notes.

So I looked at the statement and read it again, "One thousand, five hundred and sixty-four."

"That's one thousand . . . ," she said leaving the end hanging.

I completed it, ". . . five hundred sixty-four."

Dr. Shiff looked at me, and in her gentle voice she asked, "Fred, are you a reverse reader?"

I was stunned. Nobody had asked me that before.

"How did you know?" I asked.

"It's right there. Look at the statement," she said. "You read, 'One thousand, five hundred sixty-four' every time."

I looked and that was what I saw, 1-5-6-4. Then something that I could not explain occurred. It might have been that the digits reverted to their rightful places or that my brain refreshed itself but suddenly I was able to see the figures as 1-6-5-4.

Dr. Daphne Shiff at York University in Toronto was the first person to independently discover that I was dyslexic.

The other event occurred at the Department of Instructional Aid Resources. I returned to the department after obtaining the Master's Degree in Instructional Technology from Sir George Williams University in Montreal. The Department was small, so the Secretary to the Director provided the clerical support I needed. I was standing at her desk as she read my handwritten letter when she looked up at me, and in a demeaning tone said, "You mean to say a big man like you with a Master's Degree can't spell a simple word such as 'meant'?" I had spelt it "ment." How else should it be spelt?

Feeling humiliated, I turned, walked out of her office and hurried down the corridor, her words reverberating through my very being awakening memories of the humiliation, ridicule and abuse I had suffered over the years because of my inability to acquire reading and spelling skills equivalent to my intellectual level. I closed the door, and in the quiet of my office, I took the time to reflect.

I knew that I was not dumb or stupid, as I had often been labelled. A *recent* assessment done by Dr. Blackstock, a Professor of Psychology at York University, Toronto, indicated that I had an IQ of 110 and that I performed among the top ten percent of the population. In clerical skills, however, my performance was assessed at twenty-three percent, barely above the score of an idiot. Dr. Blackstock *considered* my results to be a clear indication of a classic case of dyslexia. He was fascinated by the manifestations of my brain activity, especially my ability to write with both hands simultaneously, one hand effortlessly mirroring the other. He expressed the desire to study my brain.

"You are welcome to have it … after I die," I told him.

I could do many things well, but it was that twenty-three percent, the things I did poorly, that kept haunting me. There in the quiet of my office I vowed that I would never be subjected to such humiliation again. I would let everyone know that I was dyslexic and that I could not read or spell commensurate with my intellectual ability, educational level, and *academic* accomplishments.

At York University, I was the Media Coordinator in the Department of Instructional Aid Resources with a cross appointment as a Course Director in the Faculty of Education where Special Education was one of the areas of concentration. Dr. Joan Bowers was the Director of the Special Education programme. Sometime after the two incidents I was in conversation with Dr. Bowers. I told her that I was dyslexic and I related some of my experiences. She got very interested and asked me if I would be willing to share my experience with her class. I agreed so here I was facing this large group of motivated teachers.

CHAPTER 2

THE BEGINNING

To better understand my story, I should first outline the circumstances of my birth. My father was a bright young man from Charlotteville, Tobago where he started his career as a schoolteacher. He was highly regarded by the villagers, but circumstances forced him to alter his career path.

On one of my visits to my father's village, an elderly villager, on discovering my lineage, remarked, "You don't know how proud your father made Charlotteville when he came first in the Sanitary Inspector Exam. Not first in Tobago…first in the British Commonwealth, on which the sun never set." He went on to tell me that up to that day, when someone said "Teacher Gerald said so" or "I learned that from Teacher Gerald," it carried enough authority to bring an end to many *arguments*.

My father was a male chauvinist. He forbade my mother from leaving the house after he had gone to work. She was not permitted to go to the shop to buy anything she needed unless she had first informed him of her intention. He was right-handed.

My mother, on the other hand, was left-handed. Her parents had tried to convert her into becoming a right-hander but succeeded only in getting her to write with her right hand. They were forced to abandon their mission when they realized that her right hand could not control the spoon with which she ate her meals.

My mother's formal education ended at just about Standard Five, but she had an intuitive ability that I have not seen equalled. She told me that she saw things in her mind's eye. I suspected that she was dyslexic, for she never read for information or pleasure, her reading being restricted to her Bible and a few religious *tracts*. She delegated the handling of all her correspondence to her children as soon as we were *old enough* to handle them.

My earliest recollection of Mummy seeing things in her mind's eye occurred when I was about four years old. Samuel, my older brother, was critically ill. Samuel was making no improvement despite Dr. Tracey's medical intervention. Dr. Tracey told my parents that there was nothing more he could do for Samuel. He advised them that they should be prepared to bury him. Mummy and Daddy argued over the place that they should bury him. Mummy wanted to bury him in our family's plot in San Fernando while Daddy thought that he should be buried in Couva. They just could not agree on the place where he should be buried.. Finally Mummy said, "Since we can't decide where to bury him, we're not going to bury him at all." She told me that on saying that, it suddenly became clear in her mind's eye that Samuel should be drinking what the goats that we reared were eating.

Mummy acted on her intuition and went out to gather the hibiscus, cosamaho[1] and the other shrubs she had seen the goats eat. She boiled them together and gave Samuel the concoction to drink. The results were incredible. It did not take long for Samuel to make a full and complete recovery. After his recovery, Samuel recounted his out-of-body experience. He said that all during the episode he was floating around the room. He was looking down from the *ceiling* and seeing everyone fussing around him. He tried to tell them that things would be all right but no one listened.

On another occasion, my sister Ruth was so ill and weak that she could not even raise her hand to drive away the fly sitting on her lip. Miss Kirby, the next-door neighbour, said, on observing Ruth's condition,

"Miss Thornhill, I think you're going to lose this child."

Mummy recounted that at that moment she saw clear in her mind's eye what she had to do: apply heat to Ruth's front and back. With Miss Kirby's assistance, they boiled water, heated towels and placed them on Ruth's chest and back. By mid-afternoon the little girl, whom Miss Kirby thought would have been lost, was a happy child playing around the house.

The birth of my parents' first child, Samuel, pleased Daddy very much. As Samuel developed, it was clear that he was very bright, and this pleased Daddy even more. But it was quite evident that Samuel was left-handed like his mother, which displeased Daddy.

Father and son developed a close bond. Daddy utilized his teaching skills and began to fashion Samuel's academic development. From an early age, Samuel was reading fluently. Daddy, who was a travelling officer, took Samuel with him wherever he could. They had a good thing going. Daddy was teaching Samuel everything he knew. Samuel was even learning to treat Mummy similar to the way Daddy did, much to her annoyance. She was powerless to do anything about it, as Samuel was the apple of his father's eye.

Then I was born. Both Daddy and Samuel were ill prepared for the arrival of the second child of the same sex. To Samuel, I was intruding into what was his exclusive domain, and to Daddy, I was a dig at his manhood, since I showed tendencies of being left-handed like my mother.

Although he never seemed to come to terms with it, Samuel accepted my arrival a little better than did our neighbour, Mack, when he was faced with a similar situation. When his younger brother Linton was born, Mack said,

"You come too. I'm going to kill you."

One day when Linton was asleep in his crib, Mack piled it full, burying Linton beneath the clothes that his mother had recently washed. He would have stifled Linton and achieved his objective but for his mother's timely intervention. Samuel never took his objection to my presence to such an extent, but we never got along.

I was developing as a normal healthy baby, but Daddy determined that both his boys could not be left-handed like their mother, so he immediately resolved to convert me into a right-hander.

Handedness is normally a seamless development. The dominant hand asserts itself before the baby is conscious of its surroundings. I, however, was a little boy learning to play cricket and I had no dominant hand. With no dominant hand established, crossover was not taking place. When the ball came at me on the left, I picked it up and threw it with my left hand. When it came at me on the right, I simply used that hand. Sometimes when the ball was coming straight at me, I would be confused, not knowing which hand to use. My confusion was often the source of laughter and merriment to my playmates.

It would not have been problematic if this anomaly had been confined to the playground, but it raised its ugly head when I began my formal schooling.

Long before my first day at school my father had given up on me, since despite his efforts, my interest in books was limited to pictures.

Samuel, however, had become an avid reader and would pose questions from the material he had read. They were always engaged in conversation whenever Daddy took us out for drives, but I found sleeping in the car more pleasurable.

Daddy's efforts to teach me to read failed. When Samuel began to squint as he read it was easy for Daddy to recognize that Samuel was having problems seeing the text but it was hard for him to understand that my crying whenever he tried to teach me to read was an indication that I was having difficulty perceiving printed words. To him Samuel was bright. I was just dumb. Daddy was convinced that my *academic* future was bleak. To prepare Mummy for what he saw as inevitable, he said to her,

"Fred is a dummy. He can't learn to read, man, he won't learn anything. He isn't going to amount to much."

My negative response to his efforts to teach me to read had already convinced him that without reading I had no positive future. He believed that the ability to acquire reading skills was positively linked to intelligence. Since I was displaying no interest in or aptitude for acquiring those skills, I therefore possessed little intellectual ability in his estimation. He was convinced that later in life I would most likely drop out school and find employment in some menial job to *eke* out a marginal livelihood.

Long before I ever darkened the doors of a schoolroom my inability to learn to read as quickly and easily as Samuel had done, confirmed in my father's mind that I was truly a dummy. Had I been dependent on him for my education, his words would have been prophetic. He was so convinced of my limited intellectual aptitude that he did not waste his time and energy trying to teach me.

Daddy's pronouncement and his lack of interest in teaching me caused Mummy to affirm,

"I did not make any dummy. I will do everything I can to ensure that Fred learns. He will succeed."

Mummy always remained faithful to her resolve. She tried to give me a head start by introducing me to mathematics before I started my formal schooling. She was the first of four women who were responsible for laying the foundation on which my academic success was built.

CHAPTER 3

BALMAIN C. M. SCHOOL

I remember my first day at Balmain C. M. School. It was September 1, 1941, and I was a big boy then, just three days short of my fifth birthday. I was all excited at the prospect of going to school. Mummy dressed me in my stiffly starched and ironed blue shirt and khaki pants. On my feet were grey socks and a pair of black Bata shoes, and over my shoulder was slung a book bag that held my J. O. Cutteridge *First Primer Reading Book*, a single line copybook, a lead pencil and an eraser. I was well equipped for my adventure into formal learning.

Mummy placed me in the care of two older girls who took charge of me and proudly escorted me to school. We walked up the road past Mr. Hackett's blacksmith shop, and then at Miss Mary's shop we turned into School *Road*. Balmain C. M. School stood at the end of School Road. As we approached the dilapidated wooden building that served as our schoolhouse, Miss Baxter, the entry class teacher, leaned out the window and with a beaming smile announced,

"We're welcoming another Thornhill here today."

Samuel was performing well and progressing effortlessly through school. A few years later he demonstrated the ease with which he was mastering academic challenges. The year he wrote the Government Exhibition, the annual assessment exam for entry into secondary school, he placed fourth. Of all the children who wrote the exam from all the schools in Trinidad and Tobago only three scored higher marks than he did. I was expected to follow in his footsteps. But an easy passage through elementary and secondary schools was not in the cards for me.

The old school house was divided into the Infants and Standards Departments. In the Standards Department, the desks and other furniture were strategically positioned on a creaky, springy wooden floor with large cracks, which hungrily ate any pen or pencil that might fall from the hand of an unsuspecting child. In the Infant Department, the furniture was arranged on the ground—literally. This dilapidated structure was subsequently rebuilt.

The students in the Infant Department were separated into two classes. Miss Baxter was the teacher responsible for the First Stage Class. Her table was positioned just inside the door and in the front of two low tables with four matching benches with backrests around each table. There were pictures and posters adorning the walls. An old cupboard with a broken hinge and a door that could not be locked stood in the corner behind Miss Baxter's table. There was no need for a lock since no one would steal anything from the cupboard in which she kept *plasticine*, crayons, pencils, chalk, crown cork sets and other supplies. I joined the boys who sat together on the benches on the boys' sides of the tables while the girls sat on their sides. Here I began my formal schooling where it soon became apparent that I was destined to both exceed and fall short of expectations.

Arithmetic concepts were easy for me to grasp, but reading, writing, spelling and simple instructions such as turn left or right proved to be quite challenging.

The education system is predicated on the false assumption that every child is able to acquire competent reading skills. When this does not happen, efforts are made to alter the child, not the system, because of the importance educators have placed on reading since the ability to read is seen as essential in modern society. The truth is that no matter how essential it might seem to be, there *is* no skill that all human beings can acquire with competence—not even reading.

What a child needs for mental stimulation and intellectual growth is information—not reading skills. Reading is an easy way for individuals to access information stored in print, but when a child displays difficulty with or inability to acquire reading skills, alternative methods ought to be found to provide the information needed for mental stimulation and intellectual growth. The time spent forcing me to acquire reading skills and punishing my failure never achieved the desired effect. My eyes were unable to initiate the effective transfer of information from the printed page to the brain. To me reading was and still is a frustrating, tiring process that yields little return.

I was fortunate that Miss Baxter, a slim attractive young lady, the love of my boyhood life, never mistook my challenges with reading, writing and spelling as indicative of my intellectual inability as my father had done.

I was happy to be in school and I soon got to know the boys in the class. There were Telbot, Dingolay, Ronald and Romie but my friends were Hendrick, Kendrick and Desmond. Our names followed each other in the roll book, and at roll call, Miss Baxter would call out our names, "Hendrick, Kendrick, Desmond, Fred," and in *turn*, we would each respond by saying, "Present, Miss."

Miss Baxter filled our day with enjoyable activities. We sang, "Inky Pinky Spider," "Row, Row, Row Your Boat" and the Hindi chorus *"Pyahr khar tah moodj."* We slept. We recited nursery rhymes. We did the "Hands up, hands out, hands down," and the "Mark time, left right, left right, forward march." All that was easy, but I had difficulty with the "left turn" and "right turn". In fact, I was having difficulty with the concept of left and right.

As my schooling progressed, the difficulties I was experiencing on the playground began to manifest themselves in the classroom, but unlike the playground, they were no longer laughing matters.

Writing was one of the first skills we were taught. My classmates seemed to progress effortlessly, but to me it was very challenging. Miss Baxter had joined in the attempt to make me into a right-hander, and this added to my distress. I can still remember the difficulty I encountered learning to form letters. Miss Baxter held my hand and assisted me as I struggled to form them. My actions were never free flowing, but always calculated and slow. I had difficulty getting my pencil to stay on the line, and when I did manage it, I often confused the direction in which I should move the pencil to form the letters.

In her neat and attractive handwriting, Miss Baxter wrote sentences on the blackboard and instructed us to copy them. My classmates took up their pencils and began the assignment while I sat staring at my open copybook. If the copybook was positioned straight in front of me, no hand wanted to assume the responsibility. When the book was tilted to the left, my right hand assumed dominance, but when it was tilted to the right, my left hand took over. But I was faced with a serious *dilemma*. Miss Baxter's *insistence* that I write with my right hand compounded my problem. I did not know which one was my right hand.

In my attempt to resolve my problem I asked my friend Hendrick how he determined the difference between left and right. His answer contained words I heard for the first, but not the last time, and even now, as I write this, I can feel the tears welling in my eyes because of the pain and humiliation they caused me over the years:

"Fred, yuh too stupid," he said. "Everybody know yuh does write with your right hand."

It was the first time that I was described in that manner but it would not be the last. What was easy for him was difficult for me. I could write with either hand. Did that mean that I had two right hands? How and when did my left hand *disappear*? If I still had a left and a right hand, I needed to find some other method to differentiate them. I discovered that my small pox vaccination, which had become infected when it was administered (and subsequently almost killed me), was now raised and prominent on my left arm. I could use that to determine my left hand. The need to go through this checking process made me much slower in carrying out any instruction that required knowledge of left and right.

While this did not hold true for my classmates, since *choosing* the hand with which they would write was a reflex action, writing required that I had knowledge of left and right. I was instructed to use my right hand for writing when either hand was capable of performing the task. The choice of the hand I should use for writing was not left to me.

Miss Baxter constantly circled around the class like a mother hen protecting her brood, and just as an errant chick would feel the peck of its mother beak on its back, so too would I come under the lash of Miss Baxter's whip if I were to use what to her was the wrong hand. She would also be very displeased if I formed my letters backward.

I had to make conscious decisions before I could comply with the simple instruction, "Copy the sentence from the board," which presented no difficulty to my classmates. I first had to make a decision as to which was the appropriate hand to use. I was therefore much slower than my classmates were in performing what seemed to them and my teacher, as being a very simple task.

Miss Baxter was an excellent teacher despite the fact that she punished me if I wrote with my left hand. She recognized that I was constantly getting into distress as I tried to navigate the treacherous sea of formal education. To assist me with writing she used a red pencil to highlight the left margin and to rule every fourth line down to the middle of each page in my copybook. She instructed me to start at the red margin and to form my letters between the lines that were not ruled in red. This structuring was of great assistance to me. Over time, although speed was never one of my assets, I was able to develop a very neat handwriting.

My classmates and I were all taught to write. I later became aware that they could only write the way they were taught. With me it was different. By learning to write, I was able to perform that task with either hand and in any direction. I had no difficulty writing backwards, especially with my left hand. In fact writing backwards with my left hand was something I did so effortlessly that it felt it as being the correct direction in which to write. Subsequently I discovered that I could also write with both hands at the same time, one mirroring the other. From time to time my friends would decide to see which one of us could write backwards the best. While I could never read or spell better than they could, none of them could write backwards better or quicker than me. It would seem that some block in my classmates' brains prevented them from acquiring these unnecessary skills. In my case, this block was non-functional so I acquired skills I did not need and this contributed to the difficulty I was experiencing with reading and *spelling*.

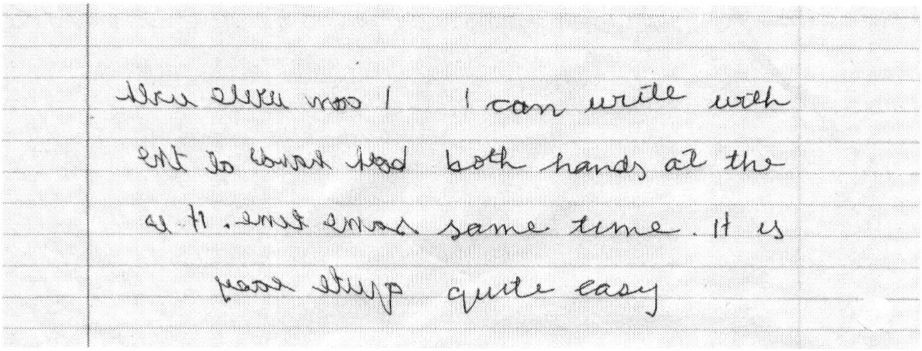

ILLUSTRATION 1

Example of my writing with both hands at the same time. Hold the text in front of a mirror to read the reverse writing.

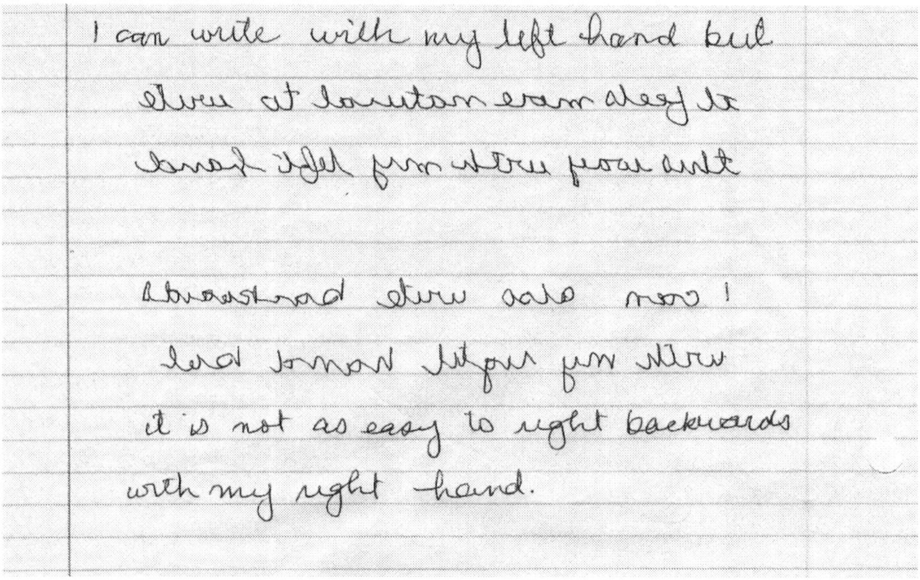

ILLUSTRATION 2

Examples of writing normally and backwards interchangeable with my left and right hands. Hold the text in front of a mirror to be able to read the information. Note 'right' for 'write'.

Reading was my next major challenge. I dreaded the reading periods, and it was there I heard that phrase again, "Boy, yuh too stupid. Yuh holding the book upside down." It did not matter how I held the book. The result was the same. I just could not master reading. Reading was extremely difficult.

"Get out your reading books" was enough to strike fear in my heart, for I knew that the letters would play their games with me. Although she was a dedicated and caring teacher, Miss Baxter's patience sometimes ran thin, especially when I was struggling with the same word we had encountered and mastered earlier in the passage. The tricks the letters played *with* me were causing me to develop a close but unwanted relationship with her whip. How was she to know that the same word often presented itself differently each time I looked at it? If the letters in the words would only remain constant, it would be much easier for me to read. I was trying as hard as I could. After all, I was in love with Miss Baxter and desperately wanted to please her, but no matter how hard I tried, success in reading was always just beyond my reach.

At this stage of my life, words were individual letters strung randomly together in no consistent or predictable order. In my world, the letters in the words took the liberty to move around at will. When presented with the word "put" and I spelt it T-U-P it was only because that was how my brain interpreted the information that my eyes saw when they looked at the letters P-U-T. I was having difficulty with the letters maintaining their order. The letters remained static to the other children, but not so to me. The big problem was that I never could tell when or how they would move. I did not have enough knowledge and information to give me a cue if I called the letters in a word wrong.

As far as I was concerned, *it* was unnecessary for words to make sense when I was reading them. I was just trying to call words, which had no need to convey meaning, and therefore there was no need for them to make any sense. I was learning how to call words when they were written on a page and not how to read to obtain information. In speaking, however, words had power and needed to make sense, for then they held meaning and conveyed information.

Every day each child had to read an assigned passage. One by one, Miss Baxter called us to her table to read the passage. After reading the passage successfully, she assigned the next passage. In this way, each child progressed through the reading book. I was the only one who seemed to be encountering enormous difficulty. Hendrick and Kendrick were well advanced in their books while I was still at the beginning of mine. Miss Baxter had long recognized that not only was reading a Herculean task for me, but the length of the assigned passages was also presenting a severe challenge, so she reduced the length of the passages she assigned to me.

Miss Baxter worked with me at school and Mummy took over when I got home. Mummy developed a routine. On afternoons, she provided me with something to eat. I loved to snack on the sweet potato or turn fig[3] that I roasted in the arch of the coal pot. Then Mummy allowed me time to play, but all too soon, it would finally come—the call I hated most:

"Fred, it's time to come in and do your reading. Sit down by the table and read your lesson. If you don't know a word, ask me."

Mummy's voice turned my sprightly legs into pillars of lead as I dragged myself inside. Tears would be flowing down my cheeks by the time I finally got my reading book out of my school *bag*.

"Yuh want something to cry for?" Mummy would ask. "I'll give yuh something to cry for."

After getting "something to cry for," I would soon be fast asleep at the table with my head on the open book.

Mummy quickly realized that her approach was *impeding* rather than advancing my learning process, so she quickly altered her method. Now when she called me she was already seated at the table with my book in her hand. She pulled me to her side and had me read the passage a few times. My reading performance at home was no better than it was at school.

Mummy tried to give me all the help she could. At bedtime, she would tell me, "Fred, put the book under your pillow. If you sleep on it some of the lesson will rub off in your head." I tried. That ploy may have worked for others, but it never worked for me. My reading did not improve. Still, there might have been some wisdom in Mummy's advice, for later in life I found that if I were *to* think about a problem before I went to sleep, I would awake in the morning with a solution.

Each morning Mummy had me read the passage again just before I left for school. If Miss Baxter called me to read before recess, I could read the passage fluently whether I held the book upside down, down side up or even with the book closed. I might encounter some difficulty if she decided that reading would be done after lunch, but I would succeed in reading the passage and Miss Baxter would change[4] me. I would return home with my new passage where Mummy waited to repeat the process all over again.

Reading appears to be a single skill, but in fact, reading is a combination of a number of skills. All the sub-skills that combine to become reading were challenging to me.

First, there must be *permanence* to the letters and words, but to me the same word often presented itself in different forms.

Second, my eyes did not attack the page in a *consistent* manner or on any predictable spot. Miss Baxter was constantly reminding me that I should start to read from the top of the page. But if reading was just calling words, which provided no information, what difference did the starting point make?

Third, my eyes moved in random fashion all over the page.

Fourth, at this early stage in my education, letters sometimes exchanged places within a word. Later, words and even lines would completely disappear. As I grew older, groups of words sometimes disappeared or changed places within a sentence. Without constancy, reading was impossible. I pointed to the letters in a *vain* attempt to tame them and to calm them down and to keep them in their rightful places, but somehow the letters always managed to escape.

When I was having difficulty spelling a word, Miss Baxter would ask me to sound out the word, but even that presented problems. At my introduction to reading, a syllable was the smallest component of a word that I was able to identify easily. I was hearing a three-letter word as one or two sounds at most. Sounding words was a difficult task as I was unable to identify the phonemes. I was sixteen years old when a friend who was a jazz enthusiast told me that it was possible to identify the sound of each instrument playing in an orchestra. That was a *revelation* to me. I could not differentiate the sounds of the individual instruments but heard only one total sound.

Since I was unable to clearly distinguish the sounds that comprised a word, I therefore could not ascribe the appropriate sounds to the letters. It was also a confusing process to differentiate between the sounds of **c**, **s** and **k**, **e**, **y** and **i**, and **a** and **e**. The problems I was having with reading made spelling impossible for me to master.

Just as she did with reading, Miss Baxter ticked off in our books the number of words we were required to learn to spell. As in reading, she called us to her table individually and took us through the spelling exercise. Just as in reading, this was another nightmare for me. Ronald, who was slow, had his difficulties, but his could not be compared with mine. Even Ronald would satisfy Miss Baxter and I would still be left struggling. I did not have any mental hooks on which to hang the spelling of any words. The words seemed new almost every time, since I sometimes perceived the letters in reverse order, sometimes intermittently and sometimes not at all. In my perception, words were not constant. I was capable of perceiving the same word as being presented in many forms, so anytime a word was presented to my brain, it might be regarded as a new word. It was not uncommon for me to come to the end of the list and hear Miss Baxter say, "Let's go over the words again," and so I would, but my brain reacted as though I had never seen the words before. I had no recall of the words in the exercise we had just completed.

"But you just said it,"

"But we went through that a minute ago,"

"But you said it before,"

"But that's the same word you saw before,"

"That's not a new word."

Miss Baxter and Mummy often uttered these frustrating expressions as they took me through my spelling and reading exercises.

My spelling performance left both Mummy and Miss Baxter thoroughly perplexed. I could remember the words of the nursery rhymes, I could recall things that happened in the past, but I could not remember how to spell a word I had encountered and mastered within the previous sixty seconds. When the bell rang to signal recess, waves of happy, laughing children rolled out of the classroom and into the schoolyard to jump and skip, to play moral, hopscotch, rounders[5] and scotch[6] while I was often left standing at Miss Baxter's table to tearfully continue my struggle with reading and spelling. It was doubly frustrating as my reading and spelling were not only causing me pain, but were also denying me pleasure.

While most of my classmates enjoyed the reading and spelling exercises, I dreaded them as I continued to struggle. Compared to my classmates I needed a disproportionate amount of help from Miss Baxter whenever she would call on me to read or spell.

Writing was becoming less stressful as my right hand became my preferred hand. During writing assignments, Miss Baxter would still hover over my shoulder, as I sometimes formed some letters backwards. I had difficulty forming **b** and **d**, **p** and **q**, **u** and **n**.

I was doing extremely poorly in reading and spelling, but in all the others subjects, I was at the top of the class. There was no identifiable reason for my poor performance in reading and spelling. I had a normal birth. I was in good health. I was never involved in any major accident. There was nothing physically wrong with me. I was bright, articulate, full of energy and everything that could be expected of a little boy. I was giving my best effort as I tried to please the two most important women in my life, but for some reason unknown to them, I could not master reading or spelling. My results were not what were expected from a bright little boy like me.

It could not be a question of ability because it was clear that I had lots of that. Memory could not be the cause, since I could recite all the nursery rhymes, sing all the songs and say all the prayers, although I did experience some difficulty learning the multiplication tables. My performance was puzzling to both Miss Baxter and Mummy, but the cause of my problem was very clear to Teacher Wilfred and the solution very simple .

"You all can't see Fred just careless," he said. "What he needs is some good licks."

Miss Baxter was not entirely persuaded but she decided to give the recommended punishment a try. It produced no visible improvement. On the contrary, it produced undesired side effects, generating more *fear* and trepidation.

In class I could not understand how anyone could be delighted and happy when called upon to read, but my classmates were. "Me next, Miss!" they shouted, jumping for joy in gleeful anticipation. Nervousness, anxiety and fear were the emotions I experienced at the thought of having to read aloud.

It had become evident that although I was endowed with ability, I was not responding as would have been expected, and thus I needed a different type of intervention if I were to succeed in the school system. Miss Baxter was the second woman in my educational life and the teacher most responsible for laying the foundation on which my academic success was built. She seemed to have determined that providing me with the grounding that would allow me to succeed in the school system was a challenge she was willing to accept. She had no training in Special Education and she never referred to me as learning disabled. She simply brought an unused desk and placed it against her table, and there under her watchful eye, I spent the first two of my school years.

It must have been challenging for Miss Baxter, but she was able to prepare the lessons for her regular class as well as subject lessons to suit my needs. She ensured that the assignments were appropriate to my age and ability. I was performing like an idiot in reading and spelling while at the same time excelling in all other subjects.

At the end of the first year, all my friends were promoted, but Miss Baxter kept me under her watchful eye, seated at the desk pushed against her table. In class, I was separated from my friends. I could only play with them at recess. My friends were in Teacher Wilfred's class, but I had Miss Baxter to look after me. I became very attached to her. I walked up the road to meet her and together we would proceed to school. When she chose to ride her bicycle, I sat on the carrier and we made our way to school. In the classroom, the dichotomy between my extreme underperformance in reading and spelling and high performance in all the others subjects was becoming more pronounced.

At home, Mummy recognized how frustrating reading and spelling were to me. She did her best to assist me and to keep the fun in learning. She tried to be playful and pleasant whenever she engaged me in reading and spelling exercises. She created mnemonic devices to assist me with spelling. To spell "saucer" she suggested that I simply asked, "SA you see ER?"

Both Mummy and Miss Baxter were convinced that laziness and carelessness were not the reasons for the poor results I was displaying in reading and spelling. It was obvious that I was expending the effort without reaping the expected return. They were unable to identify the cause, but they were determined to provide me with the best learning environment that they possibly could.

Mummy was ensuring that I learn life skills as well. She interrupted my play to teach me how to sew, to make buttonholes, to wash clothes, to cook and to bake. I enjoyed baking most. She assigned me domestic tasks like scrubbing the floors, and sent me on errands around the village. Mummy became concerned when she observed the way I responded after she outlined all the chores she wanted me to do. I would complete one or two chores then seem at a loss, confused as to what I should do next. Mummy was perplexed. I was neither lazy nor did I *shirk* responsibility, but my chores were incomplete, despite the fact that I acted as though I had completed them all. Mummy was very intuitive. She recognized that I was being challenged by the process, and so she devised a workable solution. She *assigned* me one or two chores at a time and said, "When you finish, come back and I'll tell you what else I want you to do."

One day Mummy was talking to Old Miss Griffith when I came running back *from* completing an errand to the shop. I greeted Miss Griffith and waited for Mummy to tell me what I should do next.

Old Miss Griffith looked at me and observed,

"Boy, you're full of energy," and turning to Mummy she said, "You have a very helpful boy here."

"Fred is a good child and I can depend on him," she said, and seizing the opportunity to share her concern continued, "But he not doing so good in school at all."

"How yuh mean?"

"He's always writing backwards, he can't spell and he don't know how to read."

"Don't worry, Miss Thornhill, plenty little boys do that. They make letters backwards and have problems learning to read and spell. Fred is a normal boy. Give him time. He will grow out of it."

She was correct when she said that I was a normal boy. She was incorrect when she said that I would grow out of my difficulty. What has happened through the years, however, is that with the increased knowledge and information I have accumulated, the coping skills I have developed, and the assistance provided by modern technology, I am now better able to independently discover many of the spelling mistakes I make. I still cannot read at the level expected of me, though, and seldom ever read for pleasure, except for the Sunday comics.

Miss Baxter gave me the benefit of a solid educational foundation. How I wished she could have kept me in her class forever, but that was impossible. After two years, it was time for me to leave Miss Baxter and face the challenges of an educational system that never recognized the peculiar way in which I perceived the world of written words. I left Miss Baxter's class and became the only pupil in Balmain C. M. School to be promoted from ABC to Standard One.

I felt sad to leave Miss Baxter, but I was happy to be in Standard One and back in a class with my friends. The pair of shoes that I had worn early in my school career had long been discarded, so I went to school barefooted, as did the rest of my friends. At recess, we dashed out of our broken down classroom to fight for locus[7], if one had fallen from the *huge* tree that stood on guard at the entrance to the schoolyard and provided shade for us as we stood in line after lunch. Sometimes we went down to the ravine to catch crabs, or headed to the rubber tree to make rubber balls. To make a rubber ball we first searched the ground at the base of the rubber tree to find pieces of rubber that had dried from falling sap. Then with the nail one of us was sure to have in one of our pockets, we made holes in the tree and tapped the white sap. When the sap began to congeal, we took the pieces of rubber we had found and rubbed them in the thickening sap. During successive intermission periods we would spend some time at the rubber tree repeating the process and little by little our pieces of rubber grew into little rubber balls.

Recess was the school activity I loved most. I performed well at recess and found ways to cope with the other aspects of schooling, but soon new challenges emerged.

No one had been able to identify the cause of the difficulty I was experiencing with reading and spelling except Teacher Wilfred, who was sure that carelessness was the cause and some good licks was the cure.

Miss Baxter rejected Teacher Wilfred's notion that carelessness was the reason for my failure to master reading and spelling but she was still unable to identify the root cause of my difficulty with those subjects. By following her intuition, she had arrived at a teaching strategy that fitted my needs. Reading and spelling were done one-on-one. For arithmetic, she wrote the exercises in my copybook. My task was simply to solve the problems. She had punched a hole in a number of crown corks and tied them together in strings of ten.

Whenever I was having difficulty, I used the strings to get a better feel for the numbers. But mental arithmetic was what I enjoyed most. Miss Baxter verbally outlined a problem and I solved it doing the calculations mentally. With Miss Baxter I got all the information I needed to tackle my arithmetic without the need to struggle with printed text.

In Standard One I now had to contend with an Arithmetic textbook. When it was time for that subject, my new teacher whom we called Teacher Pip, just said, "Get out your arithmetic book," and directed us to the exercise and the numbers of the problems he wanted us to solve. In order to proceed with the exercise, I had to independently extract information from the printed text.

I now had to 1) find the exercise, 2) locate the problem, 3) read the problem, 4) understand what I had read, and 5) write the numbers down before I could attempt to solve the mathematical problem. Miss Baxter had always eliminated the frustrating steps and presented me with the *pertinent* information so my task was reduced to simply solving the problem. With Miss Baxter I was able to do my arithmetic *assignments* without the challenge of any of the five steps I was now encountering. In her class, reading was just about learning to call the words correctly and even that was not easy.

The plague of reversals had not *disappeared*. I devised a method of distinguishing **b** from **d**. I hid the top of the letter, and if it looked like an **a**, it was a **d**. At about this time, I became conscious of another nagging problem. I was also reading and writing numbers wrong.

The reversals were not limited to letters and words. I would sometimes read a number incorrectly. On occasions, I looked at a number and consistently read it wrong. For example, 4567 might be read as 4657 or 4576. The first digit almost always remained constant and the last digit was fairly stable, but the internal digits were very fluid.

It also became apparent that reversals were occurring in other situations, not just when I was reading and attempting to extract information from printed text. It also happened when I tried to record information I had deduced from mental exercises. I did a mental calculation and concluded that six times six was thirty-six, but instead of writing 36, I wrote 63. When I was told to write two hundred and seventy-four, I did not write 274 but I wrote 247.

I reversed words, letters and numbers when I was reading as well as when I was writing. My reversals were a function of how my mind was processing sequential information and not a just a manifestation of a reading difficulty. The format was more significant than the method by which my brain received the information. Recalling, recording or reproducing information in a sequential format was a challenge.

Daddy was very active in Samuel's education. I was happy that he was not so involved in mine. His response to my request for help with the meaning of words was what I remember most distinctly. It was always a dismissive,

"Consult the dictionary."

That might be easy for the average child, but it was a traumatic experience for me. The words were never there when I wanted them. They performed a disappearing trick and left the dictionary anytime I went looking for them. I could not spell. Spelling is a prerequisite for finding words in a dictionary. I reverse read. Add to that the fact that I often failed to perceive some of the letters within a word, and this contributed to the words' ability to perform their magic trick of disappearing from the dictionary anytime I was sent to look for them. Consult the dictionary? There was nothing more loathsome than a book full of just words.

The signs were clear. Confronting print brought tears to my eyes but Daddy was unable to recognize that a change in his approach would have assisted me. On one occasion he was working with Samuel, who was having difficulty with a problem. I was passing by so he stopped me, outlined the problem and asked me for the answer. My correct response surprised him and caused him to remark,, "Hmm, Fred might not be so dumb after all."

Back in the classroom, Standard One brought additional challenges. Every Friday afternoon was reserved for two subjects: spelling and dictation. From our spelling book, we were assigned twenty words, which we were asked to learn for the Friday afternoon spelling test. Dictation was a passage Teacher Pip selected from a book he kept on his desk.

The knowledge that it was Friday afternoon made me nervous and fearful long before we returned to school and stood under the locust tree to say our Grace after meals before marching into our class. When we took our seats, it was time for dictation and spelling.

Just hearing Teacher Pip say "take a few minutes to review your spelling" terrified me. I would get out my spelling book and try to review the assigned words. I even pointed to each word in turn in an attempt to keep the letters static, but try as I might, the letters were still able to wiggle about and change their places. The same word appeared in different forms. Hearing Teacher Pip say "close your spelling books" put a heavy weight on me that was difficult to bear. His oft-repeated admonition of "Fred, I hope you studied the words and will do better today than you did last week" made the weight even heavier.

I closed my spelling book, opened my copybook and waited for Teacher Pip to call the first word. He called the words and I wrote them as best as I could. Teacher Pip's calling was always too fast for me. I was never able to write all the words. Some words were left incomplete while I simply skipped others. When he was finished calling the words it was time for dictation. The pace of his reading seemed similar to a runaway freight train *barrelling* down the track at uncontrolled speed. I could make nothing meaningful of it. No one seemed to acknowledge the fact that converting spoken words into their correct written symbols was not a simple or automatic process for me.

"Exchange your books," Teacher Pip would instruct us, and we would proceed to correct each other's spelling. Teacher Pip would mark the dictation later.

The worst was yet to come.

"Who got all their spelling right?" he would ask, and eager hands would rise.

"All who got one wrong?" Other hands replaced the first set.

"Less than five wrong?" By now the hands of almost everyone of my classmates would have been raised.

"Anybody got more than ten wrong?" Then a solitary hand would hesitantly rise: mine.

"How much you get wrong? No, I should ask how much you get right?"

I always felt a sense of shame as I answered, as four or five right was my average score. My answer would invoke giggles and laughter from my classmates.

"Four right? What we should do with him? Teacher Pip would ask. "We should put a dunce cap on his head and put him to stand up in a corner."

His remarks evoked laughter. Teacher Pip was trying another strategy hoping that to avoid embarrassment I would work harder and improve my performance in spelling and dictation. Although I was trying as hard as I could the result were just not coming.

Knowing how poorly I had performed was humiliating in itself, but added to this I had to endure the jeers of my classmates.

I therefore dreaded Friday afternoons. The stress was so *intense* that I had difficulty eating my lunch on Fridays. I would be holding my belly and crying from severe abdominal pains. The pain intensified as the time to return to school drew closer. Mummy was very concerned, and for two or three Fridays, my pain seemed so severe that she allowed me to remain at home. However, she was puzzled by the miraculous nature of my recovery as soon as I knew that I did not have to return to school that afternoon.

Mummy was always checking on my work so she was aware that on Friday afternoons the subjects were dictation and spelling. She was *also* aware of how badly I performed in those subjects. No *genius* was needed to *diagnose* the cause of my Friday afternoon ailment, and thus, on Fridays, my choices became limited to returning to school voluntarily or being chased back to school by my Mummy with her whip. School would have been ideal if recess had been extended and the end of the school week came at noon on Fridays.

At the end of the school year, we were thrown a challenge. Anyone who scored over eighty percent in the final exam would be allowed to skip Standard Two and be promoted to Standard Three. Dingolay was the *brightest* boy I met during my elementary school career. First in test was the only position he knew. During crop time, his parents would take him away from school so that he might accompany them to the field to harvest sugarcane. After being absent from school for prolonged periods during crop time he would return to class and come first in test as though he had never missed a day. He was extremely gifted and became the brightest boy I knew who did not make it to secondary school.

The teachers all expected Dingolay to easily exceed the required mark, but no one expected that a boy who could not read or spell could score that high in an exam. At their meeting, the teachers had to decide on the action they should take since I had scored exactly eighty percent. My past performances in reading and spelling raised their concern about my ability to cope successfully with the workload required in Standard Three. They seemed oblivious to the fact that my difficulty was with reading and spelling and not with learning or with coping with school assignments appropriate to my age. It was finally decided that I would be promoted to Standard Three, but my name would be recorded on the Standard Two roll. This meant that I was actually a pupil of Standard Two so it provided an escape if I were unable to cope with the requirements of Standard Three.

The teachers had no need for concern, as I coped successfully with the *academic* requirement of my new class. My teachers still failed to acknowledge that I had no difficulty learning. Reading, getting information from printed text, and spelling—these were my challenges.

Teacher Jit, my new teacher, seemed unaware of my plight. To him I looked like a bright little boy and I was expected to perform as such.

Standard Three brought more of the reading and spelling woes that had plagued me since I first took my seat in Miss Baxter's class. What I remember most of Standard Three was the amount of time I spent daydreaming and steering out the window from the seat I had chosen at the back of the classroom. Teacher Jit was in front of the class teaching, but what was happening outside of the classroom and the images I conjured up in my mind were more interesting than anything he could say or do.

There was a large window at the back of the classroom and through it I could look out and observe the activities taking place outside. I often saw birds fluttering between the branches of the huge mango tree in the yard next door while a woman dipped water from a barrel and poured it into a tub to do her washing. I disengaged myself from the classroom activity and allowed my imagination to take me on delightful journeys. The world I created in my mind was much more interesting than anything Teacher Jit could do in the classroom.

I would become so involved with the activities taking place outside or *intrigued* by the fantasies of the world I had created in my mind that I would be unaware that Teacher Jit had left the front of the class and was standing next to my desk. The crack of his whip on my back would jar me back to the reality of the classroom. This would *temporarily* interrupt, but not curtail, my mental flights of *fantasy*. Teacher Jit's whip could not stop me from enjoying the fruits of my vivid imagination.

Although I would absent myself from the classroom when my imagination got the better of me, I was still able to keep up with the demands of Standard Three.

At home the relationship between my brother Samuel and me resembled that of Jacob and Esau in the Old Testament of the Bible. Samuel was interested in books and was happy reading whatever printed material was available. He was not the most robust child, and he showed little interest in sports. He was happy to spend his time in the company of his books or engaged in some intellectual activity with our father.

On the other hand, I was close to my mother. Unlike Samuel, books held no interest for me. Saying that I hated books would be fairly accurate. I loved sports and outdoor *activities,* and would prefer to be running about, jumping, climbing, playing and being physically active than being indoors with books. Through my outdoor activities I had already broken a finger, sprained ankles and had made a few trips to the hospital.

Because of Samuel's ability the daily class assignments at this small rural school were not stretching his intellect. The pace of instruction was too slow for hm. Daddy had been a teacher and was keenly interested in Samuel's intellectual development. He thought that attending classes at Balmain C. M. School was inhibiting Samuel's scholastic growth and that he needed individualized instruction. He created a learning environment at home and assumed the responsibility for Samuel's education.

I needed an individualized learning environment for reasons that were just the opposite of Samuel's needs. The pace of instruction in reading and spelling was too fast for me. I needed more time to complete assignments. I was slow at reading and slower at understanding what I read.

A healthy relation between Samuel and me would have been ideal and symbiotic. Samuel could have shared with me the information he gleaned from his beloved books. Sharing would have provided me with needed information while allowing him to test the veracity of the information. But like Jacob and Esau, we did not get along and our interaction often impeded rather than facilitated my scholastic growth.

Although I was having enormous difficulties with reading and spelling, there were stories inside of me that I needed to tell. At night, Mummy or Daddy read to us from *Uncle Arthur's Bedtime Stories.* I sometimes told my *stories*, but I wanted to write them as Uncle Arthur had done in his books. I began writing my *stories*, but my spelling was atrocious. Samuel was greatly entertained by taking my stories and reading them aloud, pronouncing the words just the way that I had incorrectly spelt them. It was not done maliciously. He was just a little boy having fun unaware that his action was causing me pain and stifling my creativeness. I could not endure the ridicule so I stopped writing.

Just as the effects of blindness are not limited to the person's performance in the classroom, so my yet unnamed condition influenced other aspects of my life. The spoken word was my primary source of information. I trusted my ear. I was having difficulty with some aspects of visual perception, so information through the eye was suspect. No one ever entertained the thought that I was also having difficulty with non-verbal communication and body language.

Non-verbal language requires the interpretation of subtle visual cues. I was having difficulty perceiving and interpreting non-verbal information. I was missing much of the information others were sending through their body language. I was often told to look at the person with whom I was conversing, but I was never told how or why. Just as I looked at a passage and failed to perceive letters and phrases, so too would I look at a face and did not perceive the non-verbal information cues that most people would find there.

An incident with Ronald brought this into sharp focus. Ronald was the miserable fellow in our class. A group of us was walking home from school, talking and laughing as we always did, when Ronald, who was holding a piece of a broken razor blade in his hand, turned to me and said, "Man, I feel to kill you."

My heart was pounding with fear and trepidation as I ran home to my mother.

"Mummy, Mummy, Ronald's going to kill me."

She had to calm me down and explain that Ronald was only joking.

"But Mummy, he said so," I insisted.

She had to explain that although he said it, he did not mean it and he had no intention of carrying it out.

Mummy was well aware that the spoken word was paramount to me. She had witnessed examples of this, including my panicked reaction to her words when she threatened to leave me at home because I failed to stay still or misbehaved while she was dressing me to go out.

Instead of simply telling me to look at the person who was speaking to me, it would have been more useful if some effort had been made to explain why I should look and how to get information from looking. I was oblivious to many non-verbal messages. Being unaware of non-verbal communication made me an open book.

Expressing the same information differently also confused me. In defining a noun Mummy told me, "A noun is the *name* of any animal, person, place or thing." I was happy in the knowledge of what a noun was until she confused me by telling me, "A noun is the name of anything." To me the words were different so they could not be describing the same thing.

Other things were happening outside of the classroom. Daddy bought the Sunday paper and told us to read it. Samuel seemed to enjoy going through the paper, but all I could struggle with was the comics section. I got my information by listening to what they said after they had done their reading.

I loved the visits of Granny and Auntie Winnie, for they always came bearing gifts. But I hated it when their gifts were books. While Samuel was delighted and enjoyed reading his books, I was disappointed and mine went unread.

Now Daddy was an avid reader and taught himself from his books; his mission at that time was learning Greek. On the other hand, Mummy's reading was limited to her Bible and a few religious texts. If Daddy had made the observation *it* would have been reasonable to assume that he had found the information in one of his books as he spent long hours in their company. Mummy did not read books but she possessed the wisdom that allowed her to discover pertinent information related to the health and welfare of her children.

One day, after my atrocious attempt at reading, Mummy looked at me and said, "Fred, you must be word blind."[8] I regret that I never asked her how she knew or where she got the information. I can only assume that it might have been one of those things she saw in her mind's eye.

This was the first time that words other than lazy, careless and stupid were used to describe my condition.

Mummy's intuitive assessment was correct. Word blind was one of the early terms used to describe dyslexia. This incident also underscored the fact that perceptive parents often have credible insights into the factual causes of their children's educational and behavioral challenges. If parents' intuitive assessments conflict with that of the experts the parents should demand that the experts prove their intuitive assessments wrong before they accept the opinion of the experts.

Unfortunately for me, this understanding and knowledge of as well as the insight into my condition that was revealed to my little-educated mother totally escaped all my trained and experienced teachers who could not get past assessing me as being "lazy," "careless" or "just *plain* wotless."[9]

CHAPTER 4
SAN FERNANDO E.C. SCHOOL

Despite the absence of any positive change in my performance in reading and spelling, I was progressing satisfactorily through the educational system and was about to enter Standard Four when my father died. My father had been aware that he was terminally ill and that we would be forced to vacate the government quarters in which we lived. He made adequate preparation for us so shortly after his death we left Balmain and moved into the small house he had built for us in San Fernando.

For me this was a very trying time. With one sweep of the hand of fate I had become a fatherless child, lost all my friends and familiar surroundings, was plunged into an unfamiliar environment where the trust and honesty of country living did not exist and my mother was *cruelly* turned into a widow. I was ill prepared for the transformation.

I will never forget my second day in San Fernando. It was Saturday, September 7, 1946 and I was standing at the gate of our new home trying to get used to the unfamiliar surroundings. I was holding my precious top, which Daddy had made for me before he had gotten ill. It was my prized possession. A boy who was passing stopped to talk with me. He looked as friendly as the boys in Balmain.

"Boy, that's a nice top," he said. "Give me a spin, nah."

So, just as I would have done in Balmain, I handed him my top. He took my precious top and ran off leaving me standing in shock and disbelief. I never saw my top again. I had lost something else that was dear to me. All I could do was cry.

Bright and early on Monday morning I followed Mummy as she searched for a school in which she could have us enrolled. Samuel was already at Naparima *College*, so I was the oldest of her three children of elementary school age. We first went to San Fernando Government School, which was just up the street from our new home, but there was no room for us. We next headed to San Fernando E.C.[10] School where the Headmaster, Mr. Victor Noel, knew my father, and Mummy realized that three of the senior teachers were her childhood friends, so our enrollment was automatic.

San Fernando E.C. School was housed in a new school building. The land on which the school originally stood was needed for the expansion of the San Fernando Colonial Hospital, so a new school had been constructed in time for the opening of the new school term. It may have been a new school, but they used the same old teaching methods.

My new school brought me no relief from my struggles with reading and spelling. My new teacher, Miss Sybil James, did not take long to conclude that, what seemed to her just simple mistakes could only be the result of my inattention and carelessness. She used the corrective method she knew best, which was the application of the leather strap she kept rolled up on her desk. On my end of *term* report she wrote, "Fred is lazy and careless." Another time she wrote, "Fred has ability but will not use it."

At home the demise of my father left my mother with a family of seven fatherless children ages one month to twelve years. Mummy needed help, and it was to me that she often turned. From the meager pittance she received as pension from the Widows' and Orphans' Fund, she entrusted me with a small portion to go to the grocery and to the market on weekends to buy food. I was the one she also gave the money to take to Madam John to pay for the goods we had taken on credit from the Chinese shop.

On Saturday mornings I was up and about from early in the morning. With the list Mummy had prepared in my hand, the small sum of money she had given me in my pocket and the basket over *my* arm, I made my way to the Central Market. The din of the market greeted my ears before its colours assailed my eyes. The bright tropical colours of the garments worn by the patrons and merchants alike complemented the reds, greens, yellows, purples and browns of the vegetables. The bloody red slabs of beef and the grayish sides of pork hung from hooks above the butchers' tables while various species of fish decorated the stalls in the fish section of the market.

I walked around the market to find the best prices before exchanging my precious coins for the items on my list. Weighed down by the heavy basket, I made my way home, pausing to rest in front of the open yard where boys were always pitching marbles. I watched for a while before *continuing* my journey home.

After gulping down a hurried Saturday morning breakfast of fry-bake[11] and saltfish with a cup of cocoa tea,[12] I hastened to scrub the floor so that I could have some time for play before my afternoon undertaking.

In the afternoon, it was time for me to bake bread for the family. I loved to bake bread. I got out the wooden tray, prepared the *leaven* and kneaded the flour to make the bread that would last us well into Wednesday. I formed the loaves, and when they had *risen*, I waited for Mummy to come and supervise the baking.

The oven, which sat on four bricks, was made from a discarded oil drum. The top was cut open and a door was *fashioned* in the side. Two metal rods were inserted through four holes to support a shelf. Mummy brought the lighted coal pot from the kitchen and placed it in the hole, which was cut in the bottom of the drum. I took a fig leaf,[13] placed it on the tin shelf and rested the loaves onto it. I covered the top of the drum with a piece of tinnin,[14] on which I lit a fire with the wood and coconut shells my younger brother George and I had gathered earlier.

The *appetizing* aroma of baking bread soon wafted across the yard, tickling our *nostrils* and springing water into our mouths. We anxiously waited for the golden-crusted loaves to be taken out of the oven. I was proud of the bread I baked. For our evening meal we all enjoyed thick slices of hot bread with a daubs of red salt-butter, which melted into the soft pet,[15] and cups of carpenter grass tea.

The boy I was at home was quite *different* from the one the teachers encountered in school. At home, Mummy saw a boy who was industrious, careful, inventive, dependable and able to function effectively in the real world. In the classroom where one size was expected to fit all, read and spell or perish, the teachers in this artificial world described that same boy as lazy, careless and underutilizing his ability. These two conflicting assessments could not be accurately describing the same person. The latter surely was not a true depiction of the Fred that Mummy knew. But she knew something the teachers did not know. Fred was word blind.

Mummy was the only person who ever suggested that word blindness was the reason why my performance in reading and spelling fell well below expectation. Miss Baxter was the only teacher who individualized her instruction method and provided me with information in a form that I could easily access. To all the other teachers I was just another student in their class, and the teaching method that worked successfully with the other students was good enough for me. If I was experiencing difficulty then something was *wrong* with me, the pupil, and definitely not with their tried and trusted teaching method. It never occurred to any of them that maybe, just maybe, I was not lazy or careless, but that their teaching method and evaluation process did not suit my specific learning need. Oh, for more Miss Baxters in the education system.

Miss Sybil James, the third influential person in my elementary school life, was Mummy's friend going back to their elementary school days. Miss James was *genuinely* concerned about providing me with quality education, but I was not responding in the manner she expected. She had tried the leather strap, but that did not yield the desired result. She could not understand why a bright intelligent boy, full of energy, willing to please, and as normal as any boy could be, outstanding in the other subjects, would produce such utter *nonsense* when it came to reading and spelling. There could be only one reason. Why did she not think of it before?

Miss James came to visit Mummy, and Fred was the topic of discussion.

"Dot," she said, addressing my mother by her nickname, "we have to do something about Fred. I think he isn't seeing well."

"You mean his eyes bad?"

"Yes. That's why he's not seeing the words and letters in his book. His eyesight isn't good."

Miss James suggested that lack of proper vision was the reason I was having difficulty with reading and spelling. She was certain I was missing words and letters because I just could not see properly. Surely bad eyesight was the cause of my difficulty. She recommended that I be sent to the Eye Clinic at the San Fernando Colonial Hospital. Deep down Mummy knew that I was word blind, but if Miss James said that I had bad eyesight, just maybe Miss James was correct in her assessment.

It was easy for Miss James to convince Mummy of the correctness of her evaluation. Samuel, my elder brother, was wearing corrective lenses from the age of seven after he was *diagnosed* as having progressive myopia. So it was quite possible that I was *similarly* affected. Mummy was committed to doing all in her power to provide me with the best opportunity to obtain the highest quality education, so if Miss James said that I had poor eyesight and that I needed to go to the hospital, she would send me to have the problem corrected.

So off to the hospital I went.

The Eye Clinic was held on Tuesday morning. I was there bright and early. The doctor examined my eyes, administered an eye test and handed me a *prescription*. He prescribed Bemax,[16] a wheat germ preparation.

The hospital had a pharmacy where prescriptions were filled. Each patient first had to lodge the prescription. The druggist took the prescriptions and called the patient's name when the prescription was filled.

I was very polite and in no particular hurry to go anywhere. I did not want to burden the *pharmacist*, so I allowed all who wished to lodge their prescriptions to do so before me. It was well into the afternoon before my prescription was lodged and filled and I was able to leave. By that time, the school day was almost spent so I proceeded home.

The prescription called for me to have a tablespoon of Bemax in a glass of milk every morning. My supply of Bemax was sufficient to last for two weeks after which time I was requested to return to the clinic. I spent the better part of each Tuesday at the Eye Clinic, whether I was asked to be there or not. On the days that I had no appointment I would sit around and talk with the pregnant women whose Prenatal Clinic was adjacent to the Eye Clinic.

I met many interesting young women at the Prenatal Clinic. Some walked with the wobble of a duck and sat with their legs apart and their dresses between their legs. They made a lovely picture as they sat on the benches in the waiting room this colourful row of big bellies. Some of their mouths overflowed with spittle.

One of the women told me of her craving for chalk and asked if I could get her some from my school. Another shared her secret with me. She was munching on a clump of earth she kept in her pocket. I laughed with the lady when she told me how she intended to behave badly in the delivery room when the labour pains came. I felt proud when a pretty woman with lovely cat eyes told me that I looked like a bright boy and she hoped that her baby would be just like me. I smiled with her but I did not tell her that my friends often thought that I was stupid and that I was at the Eye Clinic because I could not read and spell.

Although the Eye Clinic ended at noon, I was inventive enough to extend my stay to the early afternoon, whether I attended by appointment or simply because I was convinced that my weekly presence was essential for the proper functioning of the Eye Clinic.

Mummy's keen interest in my welfare prompted her to question the competence of the doctors at the Hospital. From her observation, it was clear that my weekly visits to the Eye Clinic and the doctor's prescription of Bemax were effecting no positive change in my reading and spelling abilities. She therefore voiced her concern to her friend Miss Curvan, the druggist, who promised to look into the matter. True to her word, she did just that and reported to Mummy.

"Miss Thornhill," she said, "nothing wrong with Fred's eyesight. The doctor find that he have better than 20/20 vision in both eyes. He don't need no glasses. His eyesight real good."

"So why the doctor have him going to the Clinic every week?" Mummy wanted to know.

"It's not the doctor who want to see him. Fred's going for himself. He just breaking biche."[17]

That brought me a prompt session with Mummy and the belt from her sewing machine and an abrupt end to my weekly visits to the Eye Clinic.

The visits to the Eye Clinic yielded the same result as the leather strap, and the whip before it. Mummy's was still the only voice crying out that what Fred needed was help for his word blindness. No one either heard or listened to Mummy, so I was left to navigate my way through an education system that was *turbulent* and unsympathetic to students like me.

Miss James had made her contribution, and now it was time for me to be promoted. I entered the happiest periods in my elementary school life. For the first time in my schooling, the gods smiled broadly on me. Although I was not yet eleven years old, my academic ability was judged by my performance in reading and spelling and I was not promoted to the Exhibition Class for preparation to enter high school, but shunted into the non-academic stream and sent to Standard 5B.

Now I was in a class where both the teacher and my fellow students provided me with relevant information. Here academic excellence was not demanded since the projection was that the students in this class would eventually leave school and find careers in some *lowly* trade or *menial* job. I was right where Daddy predicted that my lack of interest in reading would get me. Here the only book I needed was a copybook folded and stuck into my back pocket.

I was the wizard in this class. I could easily solve the mathematical problems and do the work we were assigned. Mr. Riley, the teacher, loved history. He told us tales of the exploits of Hawkins, Raleigh, Drakes, Bartholomew de Las Casas and other luminaries of history. I loved to hear him tell of the adventures of these historical characters.

My classmates were all much older than I was. They included Adolphus Lynch, Roach, Mervyn Levine, Alwyn Perry and Hilton "Dove" Ifill. I was surprised at what academic knowledge they did not *possess*, but the things they knew fascinated me more. They contributed to making my education *relevant*. These boys taught me how to drop my pencil and bend down to pick it up so I could look up the leg of the female teacher who sometimes substituted for Mr. Riley.

Hilton Ifill was my seatmate. He knew everything that went on in the class. He saw things I had never noticed.

"You see what Sally doing to William?" he asked conspiratorially.

"No," I said as I turned my head to look at them.

"Steups,"[18] he said. "Man, you wouldn't see nothing if you look so. Keep you head straight and when I tell you just look through the corner of yuh eye."

William was a greedy boy who was always begging for anything that anyone had to eat. Sally had a roast corn[19] and William wanted some. She had eaten quite a bit of it but there were rows of delicious corn still on the cob.

"Look now, look now," Hilton whispered urgently.

Keeping my head straight as he had instructed, I looked through the corner of my eye. Sally was glancing around to see if anyone would have observed what she was about to do. I saw her pull aside her bloomers and she rubbed the corn on her crotch. She then shelled off some grains and offered William the marinated corn. He ate *greedily*, unaware of the source of the marinade.

On Monday mornings, Hilton, who was the weekend drummer in a band that performed in one of the nightclubs, brought me chewing gum and toffee, which he got from the sailors and the American service men who visited the club. He related incidents of fights in the club, and how they rolled drunken sailors, relieving them of *their* property. He told me of the whores who frequented the club to make fares[20] with the Yankee sailors. He told me about bullers[21] and warned me to avoid them. He identified a buller who was known to molest little boys. He told me that I should move to another seat if he ever sat next to me in the cinema, as that was one of the places where he molested boys. Hilton showed me a steel knuckle he had taken from a drunken sailor. He offered it to me but I had to refuse, as I knew that taking it home would generate a session with Mummy and her sewing machine belt.

At last I was in a real class where education for living was paramount and reading and spelling held little importance. In this class, Hilton was my tutor and my friend, but Alwyn was my hero.

"Yuh seeing what happening by Alwyn?" Hilton asked, and without waiting for my answer he continued, "I know you never see nothing so, look when I tell you."

"Look now," Hilton instructed. "Yuh see what happening? Alwyn pulling up his pants and showing Dometella his prick."

Glancing through the corner of my eyes as he had instructed me to do, I saw what Alwyn was doing. He was pulling aside the leg of his short pants, exposing his penis for Dometella to see. A few days after that incident Alwyn *disappeared* from our class. Hilton told me what had happened.

"Yuh hear why Mr. Noel expel Alwyn?" Hilton wanted to know.

"No. They expel Alwyn?"

"Man, you never know nothing. Day before yesterday Mr. Tucker make a tack back[22] after school and ketch[23] Alwyn giving Dometella private lessons," he explained.

"Oho," I intoned not really understanding what he meant.

"Yes, man, he had she book wide open and he was writing with his pencil."

"So why Mr. Noel send him home when he was just trying to help the girl?" I asked *innocently*. And like a recurring decimal the words came.

"Fred man, you real *stupid*. Alwyn was sexing Dometella."

So not only was I stupid in reading and spelling, but also in these matters. It must be that I was suffering from a case of *chronic* stupidity or maybe stupidity just flowed in my veins.

"Fred, I tell you what the whores and them does do. Alwyn take off Dometella bloomers and jack she up right here on the bench and was going to town when Mr. Tucker come in and ketch them."

"What happened?" I asked.

"Mr. Tucker say, 'All yuh get up,' and Alwyn tell him, 'Man, let me finish what I doing first'."

Mr. Tucker reported the incident to Mr. Noel, the Headmaster who expelled Alwyn. He said, "If Alwyn's having sex he was a big man, and my school is for little boys, not big men. Alwyn has to leave."

I wished that I could have been like Alwyn, but I was a little boy. However, the education I was receiving would fit me for life in the adult world. This was what school should be all about, not burdening me with reading and spelling.

But Scripture saith, an ending to all fine things must be, and I was soon back to the reality of the reading and spelling school. This happy educational period was gone too soon. The broad smile of the gods suddenly changed into a wicked scowl.

Mr. Noel, my original Headmaster, was transferred to another school and he was replaced by Mr. Norman Bartholomew. Soon after he arrived at the school, Mr. Bartholomew was making his daily rounds when he noticed me sitting happily in my assigned class. I should have known that school was not supposed to be a happy and enjoyable place, especially for students like me.

"What are you doing here?" he asked. Could he not see that I was sitting in the class to which I had been assigned? Should I just tell him? But without waiting for an answer he commanded, "Take your books and head for Exhibition Class right now."

Books? What books? I folded my one copybook, stuck it into my back pocket and quickly made my way over to Exhibition Class where the students were all of my age. Here I met Miss Beulah Meghu, who was the fourth and final influential person in my elementary school life.

In Exhibition Class I met some bright classmates, including Murchison Jarrett, Clyde Earl, Montgomery Crawford and Murchison Swanson. The students in the class were very competitive. They had no time to be dropping pencils to look up anyone's dress, or to pull aside their pants leg to expose their private parts. They read books and took notes, which they reviewed and studied. Here, a single copybook folded and stuck into my back pocket would not suffice. I was now part of the group competing for a Government Exhibition. Placing among the first one hundred in the exam *guaranteed* free books and tuition for five years at one of the recognized colleges or high schools.

If I were going to succeed in this class, I needed to find a method for getting the information I needed. I knew I could not depend on books, as they conspired to hide information from me, just as the dictionary did. Getting accurate information from printed text was a difficult task for me. These boys did not *drum* in the nightclub or engage in rolling drunken sailors. They got pleasure from discussing the concepts and ideas they discovered in their texts. Through discussions with Murchison Jarrett and Montgomery Crawford, I was able to get the information I needed. From a discussion with Monty, I learned that when two trains are travelling towards each other, their rate of approach is equal to the sum of their speeds.

Miss Meghu was a very attractive, soft-spoken, patient teacher who took time to explain the concepts she was teaching. I could ask her anything I did not understand. She did not make an issue of my inabilities. She never used a strap, and neither did she ridicule me. In her soft caring manner, she did her best to assist and encourage me. She was my only elementary school teacher who was aware of my under *achievement* in reading and spelling, but never resorted to beating me in an effort to have me improve my performance in reading and spelling.

Although my classmates were very competitive, I was still able to maintain a place in the top half of the class. On one occasion, when Murchison Jarrett said I could never beat him in a test, I came first in a mini test, the only occasion when I was able to accomplish such a feat in my entire elementary and secondary school career.

Although my challenges had not disappeared, I was able to successfully cope with the demands of the Exhibition Class, except when Mr. Bartholomew decided to intervene.

On one particular occasion I aroused the ire in Mr. Bartholomew. Miss Meghu called me to the blackboard to work a problem. Although in writing I had been successfully groomed into being a right-hander when I approached the blackboard a transformation took place. Later in life I experienced a similar condition. I played tennis as a left-hander but if the ball came at a certain angle I switched hands in a reflex action otherwise I would have been unable to return the ball. So here I was approaching the blackboard and reaching for the piece of chalk with my left hand and it was with that hand that I wrote…

    If 17 pigs coast $153.00

…when suddenly Mr. Bartholomew came into the classroom.

"What have you written there?" he asked in a loud voice, and from his tone, I knew that something was wrong. I nervously looked at what I had written but could detect no error.

"You can't see anything wrong?" he thundered.

I could detect nothing wrong, as everything seemed correct to me.

Then Murchison came to my aid, whispering, "Cost, C-O-S-T." I was thankful to him, as I was unaware that I had misspelled the word. Had he not quickly *intervened*, I was sure to have an *encounter* with Mr. Bartholomew's strap. I made the necessary correction.

Because of the time of the year when the Government Exhibition was held, the new students entered the Exhibition Class before the current group had written the exam and departed for secondary school. My group was now considered 'the Second Years'. Mr. Bartholomew issued an edict that he would beat any Second Year student who came lower than a First Year student in any test. As fate would have it, Omar Sanowar, a bright young student, entered the class. Now Omar was no ordinary brain, as he illustrated a few years later when at the age of nineteen he won the Island Scholarship in Languages, which meant that in the entire colony of Trinidad and Tobago he came first in his discipline in the Cambridge Higher Certificate Exam. I suppose that if Mr. Bartholomew had his way he would have beaten all the other students who wrote the exam that year.

Regardless of the length of time that I was in the class, was it reasonable for Mr. Bartholomew to expect that I could outperform Omar in any exam? Only Murchison Jarrett and Montgomery Crawford could successfully challenge Omar with any regularity. This meant that after every test I was one of those standing in line waiting to put out my hand to collect the taste of leather from Mr. Bartholomew's strap.

But this was not the height of my embarrassment and *humiliation* at the hands of Mr. Bartholomew, as worse was yet to come.

Mr. Bartholomew reserved benching[24] as punishment for illegal acts, acts of serious indiscipline or misbehaviour such as when Willard ran *afoul* of the law and the police brought him over, or when Harry did the unthinkable of striking a female pupil teacher, or when Raymond was caught shoplifting. In Harry's case Mr. Bartholomew had him lean over the bench and he administered six strokes on his behind, but with Raymond and Willard, he had them lean over the desk while he delivered eight strokes each on their behinds. In each case, the recipients screamed loudly as they felt the sting of Mr. Bartholomew's lash. My performance in spelling was considered such a grave *misdemeanour* that I found myself receiving the punishment reserved for this category of serious offenders.

Miss Meghu had given us dictation and we had just completed correcting each other's work when Mr. Bartholomew happened by, and as fate would have it, he observed my book replete with markings indicating the number of words I had omitted or spelt wrong .

"Let me see that," he said, reaching for my book to take a closer look.

My heart was pounding in my chest as he examined my copybook.

"What is this? What is this?" he shouted. "Look at this. This is utter carelessness."

My problems with reversals and my difficulty matching sounds and symbols continued to plague me and were clearly visible in my attempt at the dictation passage.

"Said…from…encounter…man…their," he called out as he read some of my incorrectly spelt words. "This is utter carelessness. I will not stand for this. Any ABC child could spell these words. You're in Exhibition Class and can't spell 'man,'" he shouted, as he hurried to his desk. The letters were all there, N-A-M. The word was *correct* if he would only read it from the other side.

I tried as hard as I could, but the words continued to come out all wrong. I could spell some words correctly, such as 'hand' for example, and if we stayed in the oral domain, I would make fewer mistakes, but writing the word was a serious challenge. I knew all the letters, but sometimes my hand and my brain got out of sync with each other and I would write the letters in the wrong order, such as H-N-A-D.

My friends, after having written a word, would say that the word did not look right. There was *permanence* in their world so they had mental pictures of how each word looked. The letters in the words in my world were always in a state of flux. It was impossible for me to form a mental picture of any word. (I just went through F-O-R-M letter by letter to ensure that I did not type F-R-O-M, as 'form' and 'from', and 'two' and 'tow' are examples of simple words that I still find challenging.)

Then there were words such as contagious. After deciding that the first letter was C and not K, I knew that the first syllable was CONT and the last syllable was OUS, but I was uncertain as to what came between. Was the word spelt C-O-N-T-A-G-O-U-S or C-O-N-T-E-G-O-U-S or C-O-N-T-A-I-G-O-U-S or C-O-N-T-A-J-O-U-S? If I had to use the word in a *sentence*, I would just spell it C-A-T-C-H-I-N-G as my chances were much better with that word. Substitution was one of my coping strategies.

I could not overcome my problems with spelling, since what I said when I spoke and what I heard when I was asked *to* spell were very different. For example, I would say "encounter" but would spell it I-N-C-O-N-T-E-R; "genius" was spelt G-E-N-E-U-S; "dealt" was spelt D-E-L-T; "sense" was spelt S-E-N-C-E. When Miss James recommended that I be sent to the hospital eye clinic, her concern should also have extended to what I was not hearing rather than only what I was not seeing.

Mr. Bartholomew was interested in none of this, nor *was* he interested in trying to identify the underlying cause of my spelling performance, which he found unacceptable. His concern was not about creating an environment *conducive* to learning. He was interested in instilling fear, and he delighted in finding the opportunity to inflict severe punishment. On this occasion, the punishment would be imposed upon a little boy who had done nothing *amiss*. His written work reflected the best he could deliver within the limits imposed by the peculiar way nature had wired his brain, but to Mr. Bartholomew the errors that boy made were the result of nothing but carelessness.

The murmur normally heard in the schoolroom had been replaced by a silence *indicative* of the *fearful* anticipation of what was coming next. The school was as quiet as a graveyard, interrupted only by Mr. Bartholomew's heavy footsteps as he returned with his thick leather strap in his hand.

"I will not accept this gross carelessness. Come here!" He ordered and his eyes shot fire as he spoke.

The school was one large room. All activity ceased, and every eye in the schoolroom was focused on me as I walked up to stand next to Mr. Bartholomew in front of this sea of terrified faces.

"Bend over," he ordered, indicating the desk at the front of the classroom. The entire school was traumatized by the unfolding event. They watched as if *hypnotized* as Mr. Bartholomew brought the strap down from the height of his six-foot frame with the power of his two hundred pound *weight*.

After each stroke, he paused and then brought the strap down again. I did not flinch, but stoically accepted my undeserved punishment. Both Miss James and Miss Meghu averted their eyes and seemed to feel my pain as the sound of each lash echoed *across* the room. Mr. Bartholomew stepped back after delivering the fourth stroke and I straightened up and turned to face him. I was the only boy to have endured his savage *assault* without shedding a tear or uttering a cry. I knew that I did not deserve the punishment and was not about to give him the satisfaction of seeing that he had made me cry.

Mr. Bartholomew seemed somewhat perplexed as he looked down at this eleven-year-old standing dry-eyed after receiving such a brutal beating, the kind of beating that had made older boys scream. Then I slowly folded my arms and looked up into his face. My action seemed to *incense* him.

"Look at you! Look at you!" he shouted. "You're so *stubborn*. I have a great mind to give you some more," he said as he pushed me towards the desk.

In unison, Miss James and Miss Meghu whispered, "No," and their whisper reverberated as a loud command, which stopped him in his tracks. He hesitated and just stood there looking at me, unsure of what to do next.

"Go back to your seat!" he ordered, then stood and *watched* as I went back to my seat. He turned and walked across the room to his desk.

Mr. Bartholomew seemed more interested in finding reasons to beat me than in trying to help me learn and to make learning an enjoyable experience in a friendly environment. His action convinced me that he was of the view that beating would be the appropriate method for dealing with a deaf student who failed to respond to his verbal command. What other explanation could there be for the brutal beating he had inflicted upon me when my unusual spelling was just a manifestation of the *peculiar* working of the brain that nature gave me? My only consolation was that Mummy would encourage me and never beat me for spelling mistakes because she was the only person who knew that I was not careless; I was just word blind.

As I eased into my seat, doing my best to protect my sore behind, the classroom activities were slowly returning to normal. The beating had shocked me into a state of suspended animation. For a long while I sat like a zombie, totally unaware of what was taking place around me. I felt alone, confused and afraid. I had withstood Mr. Bartholomew's brutal beating, but would he return to examine my book and administer more punishment? I had been able to withstand the physical torture he had inflicted, but deep inside I was ready to break. Miss Meghu seemed to sense my mood and left me alone, for had she uttered a tender word to me I would have broken down in a flood of uncontrollable tears.

Although I resented the injustice, I refused to get involved in self-pity, so with the *resilience* of a child I was soon back to my normal self.

On the *walk* home that afternoon, I was the subject of conversation. "Fred with the iron bumsee,"[25] my friends jokingly called me.

"You real good. If was me I woulda pee my pants from the first lash."

"You lucky Miss James an' Miss Meghu beg for you otherwise all now you still getting blows."

"You didn't tief[26] or nothing. Bartos had no right to beat you so bad just for spelling."

They were aware that Mr. Bartholomew had *dealt* harshly with me, meting out physical pain with his leather strap, but totally unaware that the words they sometimes used to describe my poor reading were also capable of inflicting long lasting psychological damage.

Just a few days later, when the beating I had received from Mr. Bartholomew was already in the forgotten past, I was walking to school along with Ruthven Hanson and some other boys when we passed a sign that advertised Carib Lager Beer, so I decided to read it.

"Carib Larger Beer," I read.

"A big boy like you can't even read," he said. "It's 'Carib **Lager** Beer.' Boy, you real stupid."

He was totally unaware that whips and belts may raise some *welts* but words had the power to hurt me. I vowed that I would never read another posted sign aloud again, for previously I had read a posted sign, "Stick on bills."

"Boy, you real dotish.[27] You can't even read. It's 'Stick **no** bills.' Who would write 'Stick on bills?' You so stupid."

I had always perceived it as 'Stick on bills'.

Now God saw no reason to make it any easier for me, even when I attended Sunday School. Committing a Bible verse to memory was not very difficult. I had a week to do it, so there was enough time to study the verse, thereby allowing the word and letters that might otherwise have wandered to assume their rightful places. But it was the impromptu call to read the Bible aloud in Sunday School class that caused me stress. At such times, I never seemed able to read the words correctly. The reading difficulties I was having at school followed me to Sunday School. I heard the steups, the impatience and disgust being expressed. Sometimes I would even overhear, "Fred real stupid. He can't even read." I was unable to read the Bible any better than I could read my schoolbooks.

Back in the classroom, the boys were very competitive, and that was not limited to their academic performance. It spilled over to the playground as well. While one or two showed no interest in sports, most of my classmates were ardent footballers.

When I was introduced to the game at age ten, I discovered that the same problem of dominance, which had plagued me when I was learning to play cricket, suddenly reappeared. I had not outgrown it. It was just lying dormant, waiting for the opportunity to raise its *ugly* head. Kicking a ball, which should be a simple action, was difficult for me. No foot gave way to the other. My feet waged war against each other for dominance. The choice of words the boys often shouted at me aptly described my predicament:

"Fred searching for his foot again."

And the inevitable pronouncement followed:

"Man, he so damn stupid he can't even kick a ball."

My hands had already caused me distress, so now it was time for my feet to get into the action. Instead of one yielding to the other, they approached the task as equals, none willing to give way. Each one was determined to fight to maintain superiority. In the struggle, dominance momentarily switched from one foot to the other, conveying the impression that I was searching for the foot with which to kick the ball. This left me unable to perform the simple task.

In football, there are occasions when anticipation, *agility* and quick reflexes are more important than the ability to kick the ball. I decided to concentrate on becoming a goalkeeper. In time I became quite good.

During breaks *from* the rigours of the Exhibition Class, the boys gathered to play football. When it came to picking teams, the players in most demand were Clyde Earl at full back and me in the goal. We held these positions on the class team as well. This, along with the fact that I could compete successfully in most subjects, gave me some status with the boys.

In class, Miss Meghu had intensified her efforts to prepare us to successfully write the Government Exhibition. At home, my academic demands were beginning to tax Mummy's educational knowledge. Singly providing for the needs of seven children, now ages two to fourteen, was extremely challenging, both mentally and physically. Her contribution to my education now centred mainly on encouraging me and reminding me of the importance of getting a good education.

"I giving you clean clothes and sending you to school with food in yuh belly. All you have to do is to take in what the teacher tell you," she would say to me.

I could take in what the teacher told me, but reading and spelling lay in wait to *torpedo* my efforts.

I wanted to make my mother proud of me, so although the classroom and books were not my first choice, I looked for ways that would assist me with the task at hand: passing the Government Exhibition. Listening was the mode through which I obtained most of my information. Next to paying attention in class, the discussions I had with my best friend, Murchison Jarrett, when I went over to his house to study, were critical to my education. Then, for some reason, the details of which have long faded from my memory, Murchison and I fell out to the point where we stopped speaking to each other or visiting each other's home. Apart from losing my best friend, I had lost the effective method by which I reviewed my schoolwork. This unhealthy situation persisted for two weeks before both our mothers realized that something was wrong and initiated steps to remedy the situation. We were soon back to being best friends. I do not think that Murchison ever realized how important a contribution his friendship made to my academic success.

Then the day to write the Government Exhibition arrived, and after that the results. We looked in the newspaper and there were the names: Murchison Jarrett, Montgomery Crawford, Clyde Earl and Murchison Swanston. They all received government scholarships. My name was there also. I stood two hundred and fiftieth in the exam in which Samuel had placed fourth when he had written it. I did not receive a scholarship but that did not matter. I had passed the exam. Being the son of a deceased civil servant, passing was enough to provide me with the same benefits as the scholarship winners—free books and tuition for five years at the secondary school of my, or more correctly, my mother's choice.

Despite the opinion of my father that I was a dummy and would not amount to much; or the assessments of my teachers and schoolmates who thought that I was stupid, lazy, careless, inattentive and therefore made simple mistakes; or that I had ability but would not use it; or that I had impaired vision; I proved them all wrong: Fred was no dummy. I could learn. Mummy knew what they did not: I was word blind, but that did not preclude me from learning.

Although it was difficult and sometimes painful, I had been able to successfully maneuver my way through elementary school without any special help except for a supportive mother, the early and insightful intervention of Miss Baxter and two other teachers who cared.

I had successfully passed the Government Exhibition and that was enough for me to be admitted to any of the four colleges: Queen's Royal, St. Mary's, Naparima or Presentation. Mummy chose Naparima, as she knew Mr. Walls, the Principal, and Samuel was already *enrolled* there. But I had other ideas.

Anyone who passed Government Exhibition could elect to go to Technical School. This option was available to children whose parents were unable to afford the sixteen dollars per term tuition fee plus the added cost of the books required by the colleges. Apart from being less expensive, it was a technical rather than an academic option, which was what interested me. After three years, students in the programme moved into an income generating apprenticeship programme at Trinidad Leaseholds Limited, United British Oilfields (Trinidad), Apex or any of the other oilfield companies, the Trinidad Government Railway or the Trinidad and Tobago Electricity Commission.

After contemplating for a while, I concluded that for me, Technical School was the preferred option, as I *naively* thought that it would be void of the reading and spelling challenges I had experienced in elementary school.

"Mummy, I don't want to go to Naparima," I announced. "I want to go to Technical School."

"What?!" she exclaimed. " You want to do what? Boy, you know how much children want to go to Naparima and can't get to go? You have the chance. You have to make the most of it."

Then, putting her hand on my shoulder, she said, "I don't have much, but I have to make sure that you get the best education."

After a slight pause she continued, "Education will make you into somebody. You could get a good job if you have a proper education."

"I don't want you to leave school like me," she said as she seemed to reflect on how she left school without receiving a School Leaving Certificate. And she shared the obvious hurt she felt from the neglect she suffered at the hands of her mother, "I was good in school but my mother was never interested in seeing that I got a good education … she just didn't care. She didn't even try to get me in high school or even send me to take commercial lessons or do nursing like my sisters. For years she send my sister to commercial school and she come out with nothing . . . my mother never send me to commercial school for even one single day. When I ask her just to teach me to sew she would buff[28] me and say, 'I can't teach you nothing get away from me with you old left hand.' I made up my mind that when I had children I would never treat them so. I would make sure they get a good education. I use to see Roy Joseph clean and tidy with all his school books passing to go to Naparima and I say that if I had boy children they would go to Naparima too. And look at Roy Joseph[29] now. You see what a good education could do?"

Then she offered words of advice and encouragement as she gave me a reassuring hug, "Don't worry about your little problem with your reading and spelling. Don't be afraid. You're bright. You're going to make it at Naparima."

That was the end of that. Like it or not, I was headed to Naparima, and it was to Naparima I went as a result of Mummy's decision, just as it was through her help and encouragement that I had passed the Government Exam in the first place.

CHAPTER 5

NAPARIMA COLLEGE

On my first day at Naparima College, I was decked off in my stiffly ironed khaki pants, blue shirt and watchekongs[30] on my feet. It was reminiscent of my first day at Balmain C. M. but without the two big girls who held my hand on that fateful day seven years before. With excitement and nervous anticipation, I made my way up The Hill. I walked up the pedestrian path, passed the boys liming[31] under the large samaan tree on my left and Paradise Pasture on my right. I was familiar with Paradise Pasture for I had often gone there to harvest some of the largest and sweetest downs[32] in San Fernando. Further up I passed other boys liming under the flamboyant tree in front of Reverend Swann's house. Then there it stood before me at the top of Paradise Hill, the impressive two-storey wooden building: Naparima College, where I was destined to spend the better part of the next five years some of which would be heavenly and make me feel like I was in Paradise but at others times my experiences would be like real hell.

The college was a U-shaped wooden building. The arms of the **U** *embraced* the quadrangle where the students assembled. At the right of the college building was Mrs. Walls' Arboretum, and after that the low building which housed the principal's office. On the left of the college building stood the new two-storied *dormitory*, and next to it was the old *dilapidated dormitory* and the kitchen. The small bungalow opposite to the imposing college building was the restroom for the female students enrolled at the Teachers' Training College and in the Higher Certificate class.

The incoming students were placed in one of three entry forms: 1A, 1B and the premier class 2A Special. I was assigned to Form 2A Special. The boys who were successful at the Government Exhibition as well as those who won Naparima College Bursaries were placed in this form. This was a class of bright, enthusiastic and very competitive students of whom the college held high expectations for their future academic accomplishments.

Our Form Master, Reverend Weldon Grant, was a scrawny white man with stringy *graying* hair sitting atop a keystone-shaped face *with* a hawk nose that supported a pair of wire-framed glasses hooked behind two bat ears. He had a temper as *volatile* as gasoline. Mr. Grant greeted us in his Canadian accent and then called the name of each of the boys. Some of those names would later be called in distinguished circles: Baldwin Mootoo, George McAlpine, Montgomery Crawford, Krishna Beersingh, Deokinannan Sharma, Winston Rampaul, Seulal Sankar, Donald Amichand, Frank Teelucksingh, Ragoo Dass, Wahid Ali, Aga Khan, Edmond Alexander.

The first indication that I was facing an enormous challenge came when I visited the bookstore and collected my books. I had books for each subject, and some subjects required more than just one book. There were books for English Grammar, English Literature, French, Latin, Geography, History, Geometry and Algebra. Books, my greatest nemesis, and there were so many of them.

My best friend, Murchison Jarrett, did not join me at Naparima. His parents decided that he should attend St. Mary's College and the family moved to Port of Spain. I was on my own.

I reckoned that if spelling were not a consideration I could hold my own in Geography, Algebra, Geometry, History and English Grammar. English Literature would demand a considerable amount of reading. I had never read a book in my life, and 2A Special was an unlikely place for me to start. My recreational reading was limited to the comics in the *Sunday Guardian* newspaper. I was not looking forward to classes in French and Latin. If I had difficulty reading and spelling English, my mother tongue, how was I expected to be able to master Latin and French?

I now faced a more demanding mode of instruction. In the elementary school, the teachers had taken charge of my learning experience. Here the

Masters declaimed and I was expected to decide what was important and make my own notes. Although the two exercises appeared similar, I found note taking to be much more demanding than dictation. With dictation, all I needed to do was to listen to whatever the teacher was reading, recall the symbols that represented the words I heard, determine how they fitted together and scribble them as fast as I could. There was no need for what I wrote to make sense. I would never be required to understand or to review it.

With note taking, however, I needed to listen to and understand what the Master was saying, and then decide what was important. I had to recall the symbols and the way they fitted together. I had to think of how to express the oral language in written form, meaning, how to spell the words I was about to write. I needed to complete this process very quickly so as not to miss the next idea the Master was presenting. I was already slow at plain old dictation. At note taking, I was even slower.

My reading did not discriminate. It did not matter whether I was reading printed text, someone else's notes or my own handwriting. I had the same difficulty. I had allowed my handwriting to *deteriorate*, so this added another level of difficulty when I tried to review my notes.

When my classmates seemed to be effortlessly writing their notes, I was struggling with mine. I was spending so much effort on the mechanics of the process that I was missing important information. I found it more profitable to listen carefully to what the Masters were saying and try to remember by writing a word or two to assist me. I identified some of my brighter classmates and joined them in after-class discussions. Baldwin Mootoo was one whose intellect I respected, and so I would engage him in discussions, but at the end of the first term he transferred to St. Mary's College.

Learning to read and write Latin and French was exceedingly more challenging than learning to read and write English. I just could not make head or tail of either of them. I still do not understand what the Master meant when he said, "the verb **to be** takes the same case before it as after it." I still ask myself, "The verb to be what?" Since the return on my invested effort in these two languages was marginal, I considered it more prudent to invest my efforts in subjects in which I had greater chances for success.

In English Literature, the Master would have each student read a portion of the work being studied. Each one of my classmates would read as fluently as the wind, the words effortlessly rolling off his tongue as the cadence of his voice gently caressed our ears. My delivery would be more like the impolite grumblings of an aching stomach, which caused the boys to screw up their faces as if in anticipation of the release of some noxious gas.

As my turn to read came closer, the tensions mounted inside of me, and I experienced the same terrifying anxiety as I had at Miss Baxter's call to read. When I started to read it was as a replay of earlier scenes. I painfully and pitiably struggled with the words, failing to recognize some and mispronouncing others. I was powerless against the diabolical force that delighted in sweeping over the pages of my book, causing words and letters to change places and disappear. I often heard the steups and other expressions of disgust and derision as I struggled with the words. I was embarrassed by my abysmal performance.

These experiences were eroding my self-confidence and contributing to my feeling of insecurity. During a reading session, I interpreted any verbal utterance by anyone as meaning that I had misread something. A simple, "Read that again" from the Master, which might have been requested to draw emphasis to the passage, would set me searching for the error I had made. I had no confidence in my reading, and this was spilling over into other areas where I was becoming unsure of myself. If things went wrong, whereas others would first blame someone else, I would immediately blame myself, since from my reading experience I knew that errors originated with me.

I began developing strategies to cope. I urgently needed to develop a plan for the two subjects that were causing me the most distress. To present completed homework and avoid detention, I went to school early and copied the work of one of my industrious classmates, inserting some alterations to make it my own. During the Latin and French periods, I tried to be inconspicuous and to refrain from participating in hope of avoiding the embarrassment of being called to answer questions. Mr. Hall, the Latin Master, who was a classical scholar from Barbados, was adept at finding me and posing questions that he knew I could not answer. He took a delight in *humiliating* me by bestowing on me his famous appellation, "Jackass!" At other times he would let me and the entire class know how dense I was since I could not see the answer to his question, which was clear to even "a blind man on a trotting horse," as he loved to say derisively.

At the end of the first term, I was quite pleased with myself when I got my report, which showed that I had placed fifth in Geography, tenth in Geometry and stood at the top of the final third of the class. But the report also bore the disquieting remark, "Too many simple spelling mistakes."

Although I was facing some challenges, I was enjoying the Naparima experience. I was looking forward to returning for the start of the second term, so I was disappointed when boyish adventure caused me to fracture my right leg. Without a walking cast and only one crutch, I was unable to attend school for four weeks. I did not contemplate the negative consequences.

My aversion to books meant that for four weeks, while my classmates were progressing speedily through the syllabus, I was doing very little schoolwork. In response to Mummy's constant bidding, "Boy, take up your book," I would open one of my books and stare vacantly at the page. When I returned to school the class was so far advanced that it was difficult for me to regain lost ground.

In the final exams I was able to perform credibly in most subjects but the five percent I received in each of the subjects Latin, French and Algebra brought my average down and I placed thirty-second out of a class of thirty-five. I was promoted to Form 3A.

While in Form 2A Special I was the same age as most of the other boys, in Form 3A, the majority of my classmates were a year or two older than I was. They were neither as bright nor as competitive as the boys I had encountered in Form 2A Special. However, the class work in Form 3A was more demanding. Instead of the eight subjects we carried in Form 2A Special, we were now required to carry ten subjects, including Chemistry.

I was still heavily reliant on my memory and continued to let my handwriting deteriorate further in the ongoing attempt to mask my poor spelling. I continued to neglect French and Latin and concentrated on my other subjects. I was convinced that any effort in Latin and French, those dreaded languages, was completely useless.

At first Chemistry seemed manageable, but then we got to the Periodic Tables. From that point, I was on a rapid downhill slide. I therefore assigned to Chemistry the same designation as French and Latin, which meant that I had to find someone's homework to copy and claim as my own.

At the end of the school year, I wrote the final exam. I was very nervous after writing the exam in each subject. My classmates boasted of how they went to town[33] when they responded to the questions asked. I wrote very few pages, and because of the way my brain worked and my difficulty with spelling, my answers were specific to the questions asked. To minimize my spelling errors I tried to use simple words and as few as possible. Whereas my colleagues' answers covered many pages, my answers were usually short. Outside the exam room, I became very concerned when my classmates boasted about how many pages they had written and I had written so few.

When my report finally came, I was relieved to discover that I had escaped the dubious distinction of occupying the last place. My performance, however, was only good enough to get me promoted to Form 4B, the most notorious class in the College. The remarks on my report read, "Careless spelling mistakes. Failed to live up to potential."

I was just past my fifteenth birthday and now I was in a class with students, some as old as eighteen years old. The school expected little or no academic accomplishment from the students in this form. At the end of the previous academic year sixty percent of the students of this form were not readmitted to the school. This was the class of students most likely to fail and I was in the midst of them. At the end of the year a failing grade would mean that I would have been asked to leave the school, and that was an option I could not entertain.

The only boy in the class whose age was similar to mine was Dennie, of whom much was expected, but like me, he had delivered very little. The presumption was that the boys in this form would exit the College without ever receiving a School Certificate. Representing the College in sports was their only hope of having the records show that they were once Naparima boys.

It was much easier for me to cope with the pace of instruction in Form 4B. We were no longer studying Chemistry. In Algebra and Geometry I could solve the problems and prove the theorems, in most of the other subjects I could hold my own but I still had to contend with Latin and French.

Reversals continued to plague me and note taking remained a challenge. It would have been helpful if I could have prepared for the classes, but independently getting information from printed text remained a difficult proposition. I had not progressed beyond painfully calling individual words, which was not a recipe for comprehension. I went to class unprepared and tried to listen attentively and assimilate all that the Masters said. I put little effort into note taking. After-class discussions with the Masters were of great help, but the ten-minute break between periods afforded little opportunity for this.

Mummy now had the opportunity to assist me, as Religious Knowledge was now one of my subjects. She could help me in this subject, for there was nothing she loved more than her Bible. In English Grammar and English Composition my poor spelling earned me ridicule from both Masters and fellow students, even in this class of blockheads. However, the content of my compositions earned me praise. In English Literature conversations with my colleagues provided information, which allowed me to cope with the subject. But the printed text was central to English Literature, and reading was the key necessary to unlocking the mysteries of the text: reading, that incurable plague that negatively affected all aspects of my life—social, scholastic, religious and everyday living.

I was conscious of the need to perform credibly in Form 4B. From Form 3A there was the possibility for promotion to Forms 4A or B or even to skip a form and land in Form 5A. From Form 4B there was one of only two options, promotion to Form 5 or no readmission at all. I knew that that latter option would be totally unacceptable to Mummy.

At the end of the year, I was able to maintain a position at the bottom of the top half of the class. That was a clear indication of how well I performed in the other subjects as between three and five per cent was the highest mark I could expect to receive in both Latin and French. I was actually working with eight subjects while the rest of the class was carrying ten.

Relying on my memory saw me successfully through yet another year. The report said, "Promoted to Form 5," but also remarked, "Lazy. Waste of ability."

I had gotten this far at Naparima, and not one of my Masters had taken the time to inquire after the reasons why I, a boy who was obviously bright, would have drifted from the heights of Form 2A Special to the mire of Form 4B. No one took the time to ask the question, "Why?" Was it lack of caring on the part of the Masters or was it a lack of knowledge? I think that it was the latter.

Everyone told me that when they read, they were able to assimilate groups or clusters of words at one glance. I heard this from all my fellow classmates, from both the dunces of Form 4B and the illuminated minds in Form 2A Special. It was amazing to me that anyone could extract meaning from more than one word at a time. When I read I still silently said each word, and if it was a long word, I mouthed each syllable. I sometimes needed to go backward and forward over a word before I recognized it. And I still had to contend with the disappearing and reversing act of the letters and words.

I was not schizophrenic, but I wondered if two personalities existed in my head. When expressing my thoughts and ideas in spoken words, articulation flowed effortlessly. I could argue, discuss ideas, create stories and relate incidents quickly and fluently. I was bright, knowledgeable, confident, self-assured and articulate. This was the Form 2A Special boy.

When called upon to interpret and extract meaning from the information encoded in written symbols a different personality took control. I became unintelligent, slow, insecure and inarticulate, with the ability of an idiot. This was the Form 4B personality, and when faced with reading, it allowed access to only one word at a time. This detestable character would randomly hide words from me or change around the letters within some words just to test my resolve. The reading exercise would assume a stop and start, jerky flow. It was just as though this character was mashing the brakes in my head like an unsure driver.

I am of the opinion that the model of the brain nature gave me was different from the model it had installed in the heads of my colleagues. There was nothing wrong with the model I was given; it just simply was not designed to carry out some of the tasks it was being assigned at school. It was similar to expecting a two-wheel-drive vehicle to perform well off the road. While it would cruise effortlessly down the highway, it would struggle to perform on rugged terrain.

Like all other little boys I had been wearing short pants. Getting a pair of long pants was an indication that I was no longer a little boy. I was sixteen years of age and going through the rites of passage. I had gotten my first pair of long pants. I was a young man now. The hormones were kicking in, bringing a new awareness of girls. This awareness brought me new challenges of which even Mummy seemed unaware, and she was therefore unable to provide any assistance.

I was unaware of all the ways the curious working of my brain was affecting my interaction with my environment. There was evidence that it had negatively affected my ability to play football and cricket and had a profound effect on my school life, but it was now in the process of preparing itself to cause me a fresh round of embarrassment, derision and pain.

I relied almost exclusively on the spoken word for information and as a tool for interpersonal communication. I was soon to find out that another form of communication took precedence in sending and receiving the information essential for establishing intimate human relationships. The wink, raised eyebrows, the nod, the shake of the head, physical stance and other such non-verbal cues did not form an active part of my communication vocabulary. With glaring similarity to the actions of the words and letters in my reading and spelling texts, these symbols in non-verbal communication *regularly* failed to register in my perception. I was often accused of being proud, snobbish and ignoring people. How could I attend and give meaning to something I never perceived?

Form 5 was no easier for me than Form 4B in terms of note taking, reading and spelling. However, my classmates were recognizing my ability to engage the Masters in meaningful conversations on a variety of subjects, including topics of interest and importance to a class of adolescent males. Whenever they wanted to "kill" a class period, they would urge me to raise some matter of concern with the Master. My favorite subject area revolved around sex and the maturing male, to which most of the Masters were almost guaranteed to give some priority. To succeed in engaging the *Masters* was not dependent on reading and spelling, but on the ability to pose meaningful questions and to engage in sensible discussions. This required debating skills, an area in which my classmates readily acknowledged my prowess.

The final exam in Form 5 saw me achieve my highest mark ever in Latin. It happened in this manner. Our Latin Master, Paray Ramnarine, had set the exam. To confirm that the unseen passage was taken from one of the passages we were asked to review, he took my textbook, made a check and said, "Yes," then rested the book in front of me still opened at Passage Twenty. I memorized the passage, which turned out to be the passage that appeared on the final exam. The thirty-five marks I obtained in the final exam fell well below a passing grade, but it allowed me to stand high in the lower half of the class and thus be promoted to Form 6B.

We were now preparing to write the Cambridge School Certificate Examination. The eight subjects selected for my class included the two foreign languages. I might have gotten a mark above thirty in Latin; however, try as I might to learn "amabo, amabis, amabit," I only succeeded in confirming that in Latin, "I'm a bimbo."

I reasoned that if I were to carry the eight subjects I was assigned, I would in fact be carrying six. In all my years at Naparima I was never successful in a Latin or French examination. Common sense was all it took to realize that

I could not expect to accomplish at Cambridge what I never could achieve at Naparima.

To be successful at the Cambridge School Certificate exam, it was necessary for me to gain at least a pass in English Grammar, and success, some above passes, in at least four other subjects. The subjects I was assigned meant that I would have to pass five subjects out of six. I needed to give myself better odds.

I discovered that Form 6C was carrying Biology, and that class were being held at the same time as my French class. Four other classmates were also having difficulty with French.

"All yuh prefer Biology to French?" I wanted to know, and to their affirmative response, I said, "Ok. Let's go and ask Walls to let us switch."

They were hesitant to approach Mr. Walls, the Principal, expressing their doubt since no one was allowed to drop French before.

"I don't care what happened before . . . I have nothing to lose . . . Who coming with me?"

After some hemming and hawing, Kendrick Ross decided to accompany me.

"Good morning, we want to see Mr. Walls, please," I said to Miss Bramadat as we entered the principal's office.

Miss Bramadat, the principal's secretary, was a very attractive young woman with flowing *black* hair, a pretty face and a figure the shape of a Coca Cola bottle, a Coca Cola that would surely quench the thirst of an *adolescent* boy. Her desk was positioned in front of a large glass case with books on the lower shelves and trophies and silver cups decorating the top shelves. A door at the side of the glass case led to an inner office, which was occupied by the Principal.

"Good morning," she replied, flashing the smile that would melt every Naparima boy's heart.

After getting more information from me and consulting with Mr. Walls, we were ushered into his office. Rev. Walls was a short, middle-aged man who was approachable although he was not considered friendly. After the customary greeting, I presented my case.

"Mr. Walls, we want to do Science," I began taking liberty with the truth, "but because we're in 6B, they make us drop Biology and Chemistry so we have no science subject." Had he said it was unfair and he would arrange for us to take Chemistry, I would have had to change my tune, but he just waited for me to continue.

"Sir, we would like to carry a science subject, so we're requesting your permission to drop French for Biology."

"Hmm. I would need to check the *curriculum* to see what's possible."

"Sir, we check that already, sir. 6C doing Biology the same period we doing French. Sir, if you give us permission, we'll get to do a science subject."

"If 6C has Biology the same period as your French, I'll allow you to carry your science subject."

"Thank you, sir," I said, happy that we had gotten permission to drop French, but I could not help trying to push my luck. "Sir, I would like permission to drop Latin, please."

"Drop Latin? At Naparima Latin is a compulsory subject," he said with such finality that all I could do was to exit his office with Kendrick close behind. They might write Latin, but I was not going to waste my time. However, I had been able to improve my odds from five subjects out of six to five subjects out of seven.

My status in the classroom had grown. My verbal ability was recognized, and I was being sought after for assistance in Geometry, Algebra and English, so it was now very easy for me to find *sources* from which I could copy Latin homework. I was still afflicted by the incurable plague of reading and spelling, but

I was surrounded by readers—my seatmate, Clyde Tackoor, and behind me, Leon Thompson and Horace Bowles-Dove. They would read and we would discuss, and so I was able to add to my information bank.

In the class the level of testosterone was high. Erect penises were popping up. Erotic novels were floating around. Boys were absenting themselves from classes after lunch to rendezvous with delinquent High School girls. I listened to the boys as they told of their adventures on the trains and busses, how they squeezed and played with the girls' tottots[34] and got them in the back and held them down and fingered them. I dreamed of participation, but I would have been too bashful and shy to try, even if I had the chance. I settled for the lunchtime walks when I joined a group of my classmates who returned to school via High Street. There they met and chatted with High School and Convent girls. I returned to school having met some of the girls, but not having a girlfriend.

Leon was one of the active sources of the erotic novels making their way around the class. He read at the rate of at least a novel a day, and expected me to do the same. He passed the novels to me after he had read them. I had to find a way to convey the impression that I was reading the books at that rate too. I soon discovered that the *juicy* sections of a novel often succeeded passages of dialogue. My strategy was to read some of the text to discover how the story was developing. Then I checked for dialogue. If a *juicy* section followed, I read it. I would read a paragraph or two from a few more chapters then read the concluding two or three paragraphs. This gave me enough information to discuss the book. By using the information I had and asking some probing questions I could get the story.

I was also getting other pressures to become active in recreational reading. I had become quite friendly with Raffic Ali, a bright young boy who lived three houses down the road from my house and two houses from the one in which Murchison Jarrett had lived. In my preparation for writing the Cambridge School Certificate Exam, he performed a similar role to that which Murchison had performed when I wrote the Government Exhibition.

Raffic also attended Naparima, and like me, he was preparing to write the Cambridge Exam. He was an ardent reader who frequented the Carnegie Free

Library. He encouraged me to go with him, so I soon obtained a library card. Raffic read widely, but my borrowing was restricted to the likes of Guy de Maupassant, Edgar Mittelholzer and *The Decameron Nights*.

The library also provided the opportunity for Raffic to read the newspapers and keep abreast of the news, current affairs and the latest in sports. I did not need the newspapers, as I had devised my own method for keeping up-to-date. Mummy's twenty-five dollars a month pension could not support the luxury of a radio or Redifusion[35], but Miss Kirby, our next-door neighbour whose house was a mere twelve feet or so away from ours, had a Redifusion speaker on her wall, which was adjacent to us. The speaker was never turned off, delivering programmes from six o'clock in the morning to eleven at night. The volume was always up so high that I was able to listen to the BBC World News at seven, noon and four, and the local news at many times in between. On weekends, I sat on the banister in our gallery and listened to my favourite sports programmes, including international cricket involving the West Indies, football matches of national interest and boxing bouts. I will never forget listening to the fight between Joe Louis and Ezzard Charles.

Raffic also helped me to focus on my major objective—passing the Cambridge Exam. We were carrying the same subjects, so we would spend many evenings studying together at his house. On Friday nights, some of his other friends gathered and we played cards.

Raffic introduced me to past examination papers and we spent time answering the questions. We were convinced that some of these questions would reappear. My focus now was on having the right answers to the questions that might be asked on the exam. After all, I was not enduring these five years to emerge empty-handed. My primary objective was to obtain my Cambridge School Certificate regardless of the grade.

But life was more than confronting the in-class challenges. These reading and spelling difficulties were affecting other aspects of my life. The manifestations of the accumulation of their negative effects were now clearly visible in the way I expressed myself with *diminished* assurance and confidence. The use of a small voice to draw little attention to myself was becoming part of my personality. I was now a senior boy on The Hill, but in the lime[36] under the samaan tree I was doing more listening than talking as the boys engaged in fatigue[37] and old talk. I only joined when the talk shifted to the discussion of ideas or some intellectual topic.

In church, nothing had changed. When I was called upon to read at Youth Fellowship and on other *occasions*, I experienced the same nervousness and *anxiety* as I did when called upon to read at Naparima. I loved to sing and would raise my *voice* lustily when we sang choruses, for I knew those by heart. On those occasions I sang with no hesitancy. I was less than confident when we sang hymns, since I was sure to read the words wrong and would be embarrassed by the disapproving glances my errors generated.

Then there was the question of the election of officers for the Youth Fellowship. I avoided all efforts to have me accept the positions of Secretary or Treasurer. I would have loved the office, but I dreaded the thought of having to take the minutes, which would require that I write, and more so, spell. I was desperate to avoid the embarrassment that exposing my poor spelling would cause me. I only accepted positions that did not demand writing.

But there were occasions when it was difficult for me to avoid reading. I loved to perform in dramatic productions, but reading was required in order for me to win a part. Just as in class, the other readers delivered fluently. I was stumbling and bumbling, mispronouncing and substituting. Just as in school, the steupsing[38] and other expressions of impatience increased my nervousness. I made more mistakes and became engulfed in feelings of embarrassment and shame, for the girls were now aware that, "Fred can't read." But when the play was cast and I had memorized my part, a new Fred emerged fluent and articulate. This new person in no way resembled the idiot who read at the casting.

Sports played a very important role in my teenage years, but the difficulties that I had encountered when I was first introduced to football did not go way. I had set my sights on becoming a good goalkeeper and representing Naparima. I went down to Naparima Ground and played football on the old volleyball court with boys my age. I was still having challenges, as neither of my feet was willing to assume a subservient role to the other. The battle for dominance continued. During my days in Exhibition Class, we played with a tennis ball on a small field so getting the ball out was easy. But this was not the case on a regular field, where at age fifteen was the place I wanted to play with the big boys.

On afternoons, Naparima Ground was transformed into the practice pitch for skilled football players, some of whom were regulars on *representative* teams such as Trinidad, South Trinidad, SAFA[39] and SAFL[40]. These players went through their drills and I wanted to play with them. I went into the goal, but they chased me out. I was small, weighing about one hundred pounds dripping wet, and they were afraid that I would be knocked down.

Not being allowed in the goal made me improvise in order to get the practice I needed. I went behind the goal and saved the balls that went wide, or were missed by the goalkeeper. I soon became known as "the behind the goal *goalie*." By age sixteen I had bulked up to one hundred and ten pounds and was recognized as having skills as a goalkeeper. I was given the opportunity to practice with the big guns—Willan Baird, "Big Chief" Seales, Bertrand Hills, Noel Daniel, Merle Baird, Selwyn Baptiste, "Mamma Son" Ramroop, Roxroy Ilfield, "Donkey Sense" Crawford, "Panks" Crawford, Toy Amerali, Rennie Wilkie, Hungary and the lesser lights such as Mervyn Byam, Peter Dopson, Kennie Mohip, Richie Andre and Julian Marceline. They taught me how to get behind the ball, how to reduce angles, and how to rise to collect a ball while protecting myself. No one gave me any instruction on how to have my feet behave themselves and kick the ball. I compensated by throwing out the ball and allowing my backs to take all the spot kicks.

My prowess in playing goalie gained the attention of the Sports Master, Mr. "Puss" Yamin Ali. I was soon invited to play on the College team. By the third game of the 1953 season, I had become a permanent member of the Naparima College Football Team.

The 1953 team was a winning team. It was the first Naparima College Football Team to defeat Presentation College in an intercollegiate game and capture the Cutteridge Cup. The team was very popular. After we received our winning medals at Graduation, Carl Osborne, our Captain and the most popular member of the team said,

"Boy, when I heard the applause Freddie got, I thought there was none left for me."

But he was greeted with thunderous applause. I knew from the applause I had received that I was the second most popular member of the team, but in a sea of popularity, I was very lonely. I did not have a *girlfriend*. I had no idea whom I should ask or what response I could expect so I attended my Graduation alone. Yes, I, a popular member of the winning football team was without a date for my graduation.

Just as I got little information from the printed text, I got even less from non-verbal messages. It was many years later that I became aware that it is possible to converse with the eyes.

It was a regular occurrence that after a football game, members of the team walked up from the park surrounded by our admiring female fans. The atmosphere was filled with laughter and old talk. I could not score because I did not know how to play this game. The only language I knew and understood was the spoken word, and that was not of much use here.

No girl would come up to me and say, "Fred, I like you so, come on, let's go in the back and fool around."

Years after the fact, I became aware that many of the girls would have accepted my offer had it been given. But I could not act on information I did not have. To me, if by chance I happened to perceive it, the only reason why that girl was winking was because some dust had gotten into *her* eye. To my mind there could have been no other reason. The spoken word was my only reliable medium of communication. It was the only method I consciously used and depended on. All other forms of communication were suspect and unreliable.

There had been plenty of early warning signs for the well informed to interpret and conclude that, without meaningful intervention, I would arrive at this inability to comprehend body language. There were revealing incidents – my reaction to Ronald saying that he intended to kill me with the piece of a razor blade, my reaction of pure *panic* to Mummy saying, "I have a mind to leave you at home" when I misbehaved while dressing to go out, and my demonstrated preference for listening exclusively with the ear and failing to make eye contact.

I developed an over-reliance on the veracity of the spoken word. There are those who give credence to anything that appears in print, believing that if it were false it would not be printed. I believed that the spoken word was true and any expressed action intended. I was unaware of the importance of non-verbal cues in the transmission of the message. I seldom listened with my eyes, but always with my ears. The fact that I needed to be instructed to look at the person with whom I was conversing ought to have provided information about my inability to use non-verbal language. Mummy often told me, "You must look at people when you are talking to them."

I was told to look but I was never told why or how. I followed the literal interpretation of her words. Just as I looked at a page and did not perceive words, so I looked at a face and did not perceive any message. I looked at the face and I saw ears, cheeks, lips, hair; I never engaged the eyes letting them "make four," as the saying went. I looked but I did not see. So when the pretty girls were around, I was unable to get a glimpse of *their* hearts through the open windows of their eyes.

When shyness and the fear of rejection were added to my illiteracy in non-verbal language, I truly was in a sorry state.

Back on The Hill, I was grateful to Kelvin Ali who made it possible for me to take my place on the football team by lending me his football boots since my mother could not afford to buy me a pair. His selflessness made it possible for me to play on the college team.

While my newfound popularity as a member of the football team did not improve my reading and spelling, it got me help from my classmates. It was now very easy for me to get any homework I needed to copy. I also got help with my schoolwork. After the team won the Cutteridge Cup our popularity grew, and so did my access to assistance from my classmates, but my interaction with Raffic, who was now my trusted friend, was the most significant.

There was just about a month between the end of the football season and the beginning of the School Certificate Examination. My study sessions with Raffic continued, and he provided me with information I could not extract from the books by myself. We reviewed each subject the night before each exam, except for Latin, which I did not write. When the results were published, they revealed that Raffic had earned a Grade 1. I received an absent in Latin, which I expected, but what was more important, I obtained five Cs and two Ds, which got me a Grade 3.

I was delighted. I had given Mummy the reward she wanted. Despite my challenges and difficulty with reading and spelling, I was successful at the Cambridge School Certificate Exam. All through my elementary and secondary schools years, Mummy kept reminding me that I had the ability, and she kept drumming in my head the need for me to get the best education I could, as education was the key to a better life. She knew I could do it and now had tangible proof of what she had known since my birth. She had not made a dummy.

Despite the trials and tribulations, I had enjoyed my stay at Naparima College. I was glad that Mummy had insisted that I attend Naparima and had not allowed me to go to San Fernando Technical School. Still, I vowed that there would be no more formal education for me. I would never allow myself to be subjected to the pressures of an educational institution again. There would be no more books for me. I would get a job and work happily ever after for the rest of my life.

CHAPTER 6

THE WORLD OF WORK

The combination of my Cambridge School Certificate and my football accomplishments made it easy for me to find employment at Trinidad Leaseholds Limited as a *Laboratory* Attendant in the Research Lab. I was happy to be employed. My first two weeks at the Lab were spent in the Analytic Section, after that I was transferred to the Pilot Plant where I had a rude introduction to the harsh reality of the world of work in the oilfield.

On my first day at the Plant, one of the more experienced employees took me aside and instructed me on how I should approach work. He welcomed me to the Plant and told me that I should be able to come to work and do nothing all day. In order to accomplish this I first had to learn how to pose. Posing was the art of doing nothing while creating the impression of working. He boasted that he could spend an entire day doing nothing. He said that the important thing was to always have a tool, a sample or something in my hand, and when a boss approached, I should walk briskly, as if on a mission. Although I did not smoke, he said that I should take smoke breaks anyway and just light a cigarette and sit in the smoke shed.

I was learning slowly, but not getting very good at posing when I was moved from working daylight—seven to four—and placed on shift where I was assigned to operate the pilot catalytic cracker. On one shift, as my plant was down, I was asked to sift catalyst. I limed for most of the night, and coming to the end of the shift, I spent forty-five minutes sifting catalyst and placed the nine hundred and fifty grams into the jar. I was somewhat uncomfortable because I knew how little work I had done. The longer serving employee who relieved me reacted quite differently.

"What?!" he exclaimed on reading my log. "No man. You can't enter that."

"What's wrong?" I wanted to know.

"That is too much catalyst. You can't give the boss bad habit. You not suppose to sift so much. You only making work for everybody."

"How much I should put?" I asked.

"Put one fifty. Take out eight hundred and keep it in your cupboard so next time you have to sift you could just take out a hundred or so."

One hundred and fifty grams, which was less than five minutes effort, was all that I needed to show for eight hours of work.

Working was not turning out to be what I expected. Going to the plant each shift and operating a pilot plant was neither challenging nor did it tax my ability. I began to miss the intellectual stimulation that school had provided. To try to fill the void I became active in amateur dramatic productions. I wrote verse and created a one-act play with Lewis King. I generated the ideas and he did the writing so I did not have to contend with spelling. I was writing, but still not reading, and spelling was still difficult. Time had not improved the situation.

Most of my close friends were also working at Trinidad Leaseholds Limited. When we started going to fetes, seven of us young men went together: Mervyn Byam, Hollis Loney, Inskip Diaz, Albert LaVeau, Ben Brown, Lewis Collins the only one who was not working at TLL,[41] and me. We met and primed up[42] before proceeding to a fete. Once inside, the routine was that we put up money, bought a bottle of rum and chasers, got some glasses and ice, found a table and established our base. Then I joined my friends in scouting the fete.

The beautiful young ladies, all dressed in their lovely outfits, were standing in small groups or sitting in chairs pushed against the walls. Like books, their attractive figures and pretty faces contained valuable information, but unfortunately for me the information was encoded in a language I did not understand. When we scouted the fete, I thought that we were just walking around the hall, greeting the people we knew and then returning to our base. I was totally unaware of the non-verbal communication that took place between the girls and my friends. I never perceived any of it. My brain just did not like reading whether the information was written, printed or non-verbal.

But my friends read the messages well, for they were soon successfully finding dancing partners while I was spending extended time at the table timidly venturing to seek partners by hit and miss. At the end of the fete, most of my friends had someone to take home while I took my lonely walk home and tried to find answers to the question, "Why? Why am I unable to pick up a girl?"

My accomplishment on the football field, my verbal competence and my general appearance made it difficult for my friends to understand the difficulty I was having with girls. One of my friends who was big and overweight said,

"Man, leave that for people like me. You don't look like a stupidy[43]."

But looks were oh so deceiving.

Just as my friends had assisted me with reading in the classroom, my friend Hollis helped me by reading and interpreting the non-verbal messages women sent in my direction.

"That girl like you," he would point out. "Try her."

I would follow Hollis' advice, but another hurdle would soon appear. Alone with the girl there was important information that I could not read that indicated the *pace* at which she was prepared to proceed. Without that information to guide me, I moved straight in for the prize only to succeed in ending what could have been a romantic interlude. Without the information I was moving too fast, which had the same effect as not moving at all.

Hollis offered further assistance. He said that when dancing I should blow in the girl's ear and she would go weak in my arms. At my next opportunity, I followed Hollis' advice and tried to impress the young lady with the capacity of my lungs. Instead of going weak, it brought her to life, and I was left standing alone and embarrassed on the dance floor, which was not the desired effect.

I told Hollis what had happened, and he just burst into a fit of uncontrollable laughter. After he was able to control himself, I was greeted with the familiar phrase, "Fred, you too damn stupid. You think the girl ear is a balloon or what? It's not like you blowing a balloon, it's more like you just breathing through your mouth."

Now why did he not tell me that in the first place? To me words tell the whole story, and there was a big difference, as I found out, between blowing into a girl's ear and breathing into it gently.

The difficulty with perception that negatively affected my reading and spelling in the classroom was having the same effect on this aspect of my life. My inability to perceive non-verbal cues was making me *into* the kind of young man a mother-in-law would love because I was dependable and would take care of her daughter, but the daughter would despise because I was blind to her messages and thus would not make a woman out of her.

My relationship with my friend Merlyn was a good example of this. I found her to be a very attractive young lady. During my latter teen years, I would lengthen the time it took me to go to the shop by standing in her yard and talking with her. On some afternoons she would walk up the street and we would spend time talking and laughing in front of my home. Merlyn told me that her mother would allow her to go to parties if I were taking her. I asked her mother, who always said yes, and Merlyn would step out in her pretty dress and wide crinoline and we would go to parties. I enjoyed taking her to Sunday afternoon parties in Forest Reserve and Apex. When the parties ended, I always took Merlyn safely back home as I had promised her mother I would do.

We went our separate ways and met again after many years. During our conversation, she said,

"Man, you were never interested in me."

"I didn't know you liked me."

"Boy, you real stupid. Why you think I was coming up by you and letting you ask Mammy to take me out?"

The truth was that at that time I really did not know why.

Then there was the occasion when my friend whom we called Polecras, invited me to come along to a party. It was one of those university parties where the partygoers drank beer, ate pizza and devised solutions for all the world's problems. We arrived late at the small bungalow in one of the Montreal suburbs. We walked in and quickly closed the door behind us to shut out the cold. We stood for a while surveying the scene.

I did not recognize anyone. Some young ladies were sitting in the living room chairs that had been pushed against the wall. Young people were standing in groups around the room. In the far corner, a disc jockey was spinning records on a Clairtone Project G System. Other people were in discussion around the dining table. Three young ladies were standing and talking off to the side while a group of noisy young men with bottles of beer in their hands was milling around in a corner.

Polecras must have known the young ladies, for one of them smiled at us as we passed on our way to the kitchen to deposit the two six-packs of beer we had brought. He introduced me to the host, and after some small talk, I took a bottle of beer and went back inside where I stood for a while, and then went over and joined the group of boys. I spent some time with them before getting another beer and going over to the table, where incest was the topic under discussion.

Shortly after I took my seat, the young lady who had smiled with Polecras when we entered the bungalow pulled up a chair and joined the discussion. Her presence could not have been missed. She became a high profile person in the discussion. I sat quietly as I listened to the arguments. She seemed to be trying to involve me as she asked the question why incest was illegal. I sipped my beer and watched her hold court. I knew that I could have ended the discussion by pointing out that nature *frowns* on it, but I held my peace. After listening for a while longer, I decided to leave, and got up and took my lonely journey home.

A few days later, Polecras came in and said, "Boy, Judy say she like you but you wouldn't take her on."

"Who is Judy?" I wanted to know.

"The girl at the party."

"Which girl?"

"She was standing with two other girls when we went in and she was at the table when you all were talking about incest."

Judy and I did meet later, and this was her version of what happened that night.

She said that when Polecras and I walked in, her friend turned to her and said, "Judy, there is the kind of man you like."

She looked at me and was interested, so she smiled and tried to establish eye contact as I walked in, but I ignored her. When I went over and joined the group of boys, she tried to attract my attention without success. She saw me get a beer and join the discussion at the table so she came over and tried to show her interest, but I was unresponsive to her approach. She wanted to know if I did not like women to chase after me. The truth was that I never received any of her non-verbal messages. It was only when Polecras spoke with me that I became aware of her interest. The spoken word was my reliable medium of communication. The blindness Mummy spoke about was manifesting itself in unexpected areas not specific to words.

Later in life, I recognized my inabilities and got hold of a book, yes a book, which was filled with illustrations *depicting* and providing the interpretation of non-verbal messages delivered through the use of body language. It proved to be more of an intellectual exercise than a help to improve my non-verbal communication skills. I attended social functions and left alone, just as I had done before. In the solitary stillness of my room, I mentally replayed the evening's events, and I was able to recall some of the non-verbal messages and interpret their meaning, but alas, it was too late for me to take advantage of the information, for the opportunity had long passed.

Back at the Research Lab the staff members were mainly young high school graduates. On night shifts, the topic of conversation regularly turned to going abroad to study. Every August, one or more of my workmates resigned and headed off to some university mainly in the United States, Canada or England. My colleagues encouraged me to save my money and go abroad to study. Mummy's voice kept ringing in my ear, "Get a good education," but although I was unhappy at Trinidad Leaseholds Limited, the thought of re-entering a formal educational institution was still not appealing to me. I thought that changing jobs would improve my outlook, so after five years I moved to Federation Chemicals Limited, the first petrochemical plant to be established in Trinidad. It gave birth to the Point Lisas Industrial Complex.

Federation Chemicals Limited was the highest paying employer in the petroleum industry. Being a new and expanding company meant opportunity for rapid promotion. I was soon a Senior Operator. To me the salary was high, but the job satisfaction was low. Just as in the Pilot Plant at the Research Lab, I found little intellectual stimulation in operating a chemical plant. There were also some environmental issues that troubled me, including the fact that lead arsenate, a catalyst used in the manufacture of ammonium sulfate, was constantly being washed down the drains and flowed into the mangrove where the fishermen gathered *their* oysters. That really bothered me.

Just as the Research Lab, Federation Chemicals was staffed by a significant number of young high school graduates. Every August there was a regular outflow as some resigned to enter universities in Canada and the United States or to journey to England in search of a better life.

I was slowly realizing that Federation Chemicals could not provide me with a career I could follow for the rest of my life. During night shifts my friend Carlton Joseph, who worked in the laboratory, would join me. We would sit outside of the Utility Plant and dream of a brighter future. We talked of the need to enter university. Slowly I came to recognize the validity of what Mummy had been telling me all along—education was a prerequisite to a fulfilling career. I decided that I would enter university, but I was yet to determine a career path.

I had abandoned any thought of becoming a doctor long before I left Miss Baxter's class. I originally chose that profession based on a child's conjecture that doctors would not die since they knew the remedy for all ailments. The death of Dr. Tracey cured me of that ill-conceived ambition. Now choosing a career brought new challenges. I had to find a profession that would allow me to veil my reading and spelling difficulties.

I had been leaning towards law, but the prospect of having to read all the briefs and legal papers steered me in another direction. I thought about accounting, but visions of writing numbers wrong haunted me. I decided that I would study drama, but how could I tell anyone that I was going away to study drama? I finally decided that since I had worked in a research laboratory and was employed in the chemical industry I would pursue a degree in science.

When I began my search for a university, I became more and more depressed, as I found that university after university demanded a foreign language as a prerequisite for matriculation. Then I was pleasantly surprised and relieved to discover that Sir George Williams University in the heart of Montreal, a French-speaking city in a predominantly English-speaking nation, did not require a foreign language on an applicant's transcript. I applied and was elated when I received notification that I had been accepted.

Now I faced the final hurdle. I had no money, and to that date the down payment required for the purchase of a vehicle was the only sum of money I had been able to accumulate. I hatched a plan to get the money I needed. First,

I sold my car. Then I calculated the amount of money I needed to cover my monthly expenses and authorized the Credit Union to deduct from my salary everything in excess of that amount. In that way the money did not come into my hand, and so in fourteen months I was able to accumulate the funds I needed to cover the tuition fee and living expenses for a year at Sir George Williams University in Montreal. I knew that I would make Mummy proud when I told her that her son who was word blind, who my father thought was a dummy, would be the first of her seven children to enter university. Four others would eventually follow in my footsteps.

So in September 1963, ten years after vowing never again to subject myself to the rigors of formal education, I was sitting in a classroom at Sir George Williams University in Montreal, Canada, pursuing a Bachelor of Science degree.

CHAPTER 7
SIR GEORGE WILLIAMS UNIVERSITY

As punishment for breaking my vow never to enroll in an educational institution again, fate conspired to make my entry into university difficult. An immigration delay caused me to miss the first three weeks of classes. I arrived at school on the final day allowed for changing courses. I registered in English, Chemistry, Biology, Algebra, and Mathematics and faced the task of catching up in all five subjects.

The Chemistry lectures were held in Burke's Hall to a packed room of young, enthusiastic students eager to learn. It was necessary to get there early to secure a seat. Dr. Sam Madras was on the stage so far away from where I stood at the back of the hall that he looked like a Lilliputian. By the end of that lecture, I realized that Dr. Madras had already covered all the Chemistry that I knew. By the end of my second lecture, I sadly acknowledged that he had now covered all that I would ever know about the subject. After a few more half-hearted attempts to come to terms with this subject, I decided that it was a waste of time and I never returned to that class.

My fortune was better in the other subjects, although I had to work well into the night on some of the mathematical concepts. In English and Biology my problems from elementary and secondary schools came back to visit me. I had to quickly devise effective strategies to deal with the challenges presented by reading and spelling.

In Biology, all the sections came together for the lecture. It was a large class, but small enough to allow me the opportunity to question the professor after his lecture. This was important for me to get a better understanding of the subject. In the seminars, we discussed the issues the professor raised in his lecture. It was a small group of well-read students so my acute listening ability and oral comprehension allowed me to keep abreast without the laborious task of reading.

When I entered the Biology Lab, the students were already working in pairs. An attractive young lady from Trinidad decided that she would work with me. She was a bright and dedicated student, and proved to be an excellent lab partner. She attended all the lectures and did all the preparations for the experiments, so she took charge and guided me through our assignments. We also discussed the issues raised in the lectures and she assisted me greatly in that course. I am sure that she was sending her message loud and clear, but I never understood it, and therefore I never knew whether or not she was interested in experimenting in human biology.

In English 211, the compulsory First Year subject, we were taught the mechanics of writing term papers and book reports as well as English Grammar and the art of writing compositions. It was easy to generate the ideas for an English Composition, but to encode the ideas into written form brought into focus the challenge of spelling. My compositions displayed a systematic development of the theme, well-structured paragraphs and correct use of punctuation marks, but attracted a sea of red where the lecturer had noted spelling mistakes. In order to reduce the number of mistakes I became very *creative* in the use of simple words. But this was only a small help as I had no way of controlling the unconscious reversals, and I sometime had difficulty spelling even the simple words.

The typewritten book report was due at the end of the first semester. I did not read the entire book in order to fashion my report, but here I was with my completed book report technically sound, content good, but spelling atrocious. Then fortune smiled on me. A young lady I had known in Trinidad who was working on a graduate degree in Toronto came to visit her friend in Montreal. She offered to type my book report for me so I got my typing done with a built in spell check. Fortune repeated itself for my term paper, which was due at the end of the second *semester*.

In that English 211 class, we were sometimes given an exercise that required us to read and analyze a written passage. My seatmate and I shared our text, so we read from the same book. I soon discovered that he was ready to turn the page long before I was even close. So I just read the first paragraph and one in the middle as far as I could before he was ready to turn. I depended on the information from the discussion to fill the gaps in my knowledge of the passage.

University presented many distractions. There were the clubs, the newspaper, the student politics, the sports teams and even the invitation to drink in the pub next door to the university. Although I was very focused on attending every class, it did not stop me from participating in extracurricular activities. I was active in the Drama Club and the West Indian Students Society. I participated in a fund-raising concert and co-directed and participated in a Caribbean Dance Concert.

My involvement in the arts prompted a discussion with my friend Vernon Eccles, who was concerned that I might fail my year. He suggested that I consider switching to a programme at Ryerson. He said that Ryerson had some artsy programmes. He was unaware of all of them but knew that they offered a programme in Radio and Television Arts. I assured Vernon that I had no intention of failing my year at Sir George and thanked him for his recommendation, which I intended to pursue. So at the end of the academic year, with three Cs and a D on my transcript, I packed my bag and baggage and headed to Toronto, having been admitted to the Radio and Television Arts Programme at Ryerson Polytechnical Institute.

CHAPTER 8
RYERSON POLYTECHNICAL INSTITUTE

Ryerson was a small institution with intimate classes. Although it was a liberal arts programme, it was very easy for me to cope. I got to know each one of my lecturers personally, and I could question them and engage them in discussions. There was a practical hands-on component to the programme. The assessment was continuous and not dependent on a final examination, and past exam papers were available for perusal. For these reasons, the programme was well within my competence.

However, there were two subjects that my classmates found to be extremely easy, but I found to be extremely challenging: typing and phonetics. These two courses served to illustrate in no uncertain manner that I was never going to outgrow my reversals, my poor spelling, my perception problem *and* my reading difficulty.

Commercial writing, news writing and script writing were core subjects in the programme. Typing was considered essential for participating in these subjects. Typing was a compulsory subject, with Pass or Fail the only grades awarded. Typing proved to be the most difficult subject of my entire tertiary education career.

I had an easy time with the early drills—**a, s, d, f, g** with my left hand, and **;, l, k, j, h** with my right. I knew my fingers and their respective keys. I was happy typing the finger exercises, but the transcription exercises saw my troubles soar. My difficulties were compounded when I was required to attain a specified typing speed. Imagine my predicament when Miss Gregg told the class that we needed to achieve a speed of twenty-five words per minute in order to pass the course. I was required to read the given text and accurately type the words at a minimum rate of twenty-five words a minute. I would be challenged to read accurately at a rate of twenty-five words a minute and now I was expected to read and type a passage accurately at that enormous rate. To compound the difficulty every error resulted in a two-word deduction. Thirty typed words with ten errors resulted in a speed of ten words per minute.

In normal circumstances when presented with print, 1) I was unable to read well at the best of times, 2) I made many mistakes, 3) I read very slowly, 4) I often reread words and phrases, 5) I reversed letters, 6) I reversed words, 7) I failed to perceive letters, and 8) I failed to perceive words. With this history, how could I ever be expected to type at the rate of twenty-five words per minute?

Miss Gregg reminded me of Miss Baxter. She could not understand how a bright, intelligent, articulate young man was having so much difficulty typing a simple passage. She gave me all the help she could, but I was unable to achieve the required speed. By the final day of the class, all my classmates had successfully completed the typing course. I was the only student left in the room. I tried and tried but I just could not succeed. The errors kept reducing my typing speed. Then I experienced the descent into the bottomless pit of nervousness, frustration, anger and *despair* from being unable to accomplish a seemingly simple task. It was not just a matter of failing a course; my entire career hinged on success in this one typing course. The possibility for success was slowly fading, and as the end of the class approached, the frequency of my errors increased. I do not know who was suffering more, Miss Gregg or me. Finally, with deep compassion, she said, "Fred, you have attended every class and worked harder than anyone. Your effort has earned you a pass in this course."

I thanked Miss Gregg and left, walking out into the winter's cold. Instead of being relieved and happy at being successful in the compulsory course, I was sad and depressed as I walked slowly and aimlessly, oblivious to the freezing cold. "Why?" I asked myself. "Why?" I wanted to know why I could not succeed at typing, when back home it was the girls without a brain in their heads who attended commercial schools where shorthand and typing were the only subjects at which they could succeed. But I, a university undergraduate, could not master such a simple task. Why?

Somehow I found my way home and suddenly realized how cold I was. The warm building would soon drive the cold from my freezing body, but nothing would ever remove the cold fact that seemingly simple tasks involving reading and spelling would always lie just beyond my reach.

Phonetics was the other challenge. Here I regressed to being the little boy in Miss Baxter's class, terrified by the knowledge that I would be called to read and spell. In Phonetics we were introduced to the International Phonetic Alphabet, which was designed to represent only those qualities of speech that are distinctive in spoken language. I was faced with learning a new written language.

There I was, trying to differentiate sounds, fit sounds with symbols, and remember the correct order of the symbols. My lips would be going through silent contortions as they tried to engage the internal working of my brain. The only difference now was that when I vocalized the utter *nonsense* that I sometimes did, I did not feel the sting of Miss Baxter's whip but encountered the expressions of disgust and contempt of my classmates. The same troubles I had encountered when I was a child were the ones I was experiencing now. I had not changed. I could never outgrow myself.

Here again, just as I had done in Miss Baxter's class, just as I had faced with reading, spelling, dictation, Latin, French and typing, Phonetics, which seemed to be a simple subject to all my classmates, was very difficult to me. I could accomplish subjects that were more complex, but this was beyond me. My invested efforts in Phonetics failed to yield commensurate returns, but I happily settled for a pass in that subject.

The hardship presented by Typing and Phonetics did not prevent me from always being in the top five of the class. I worked within the boundaries imposed by my limitations. I attended all of my classes, resisting all requests by my classmates to accompany them during school hours to places of entertainment on Spadina Avenue.

I was *performing* quite well at Ryerson. Being consistently at the top of the class was the best I had performed at any educational institution. However, I wanted to do better. I became aware of Talking Books, which were audio tape recordings of literary works. Some of the books being used in the programme were available as Talking Books.

At last, here was the answer to my prayer—books available on audio tape. I no longer needed to read. I could just sit back and listen to the books. I acquired some Talking Books, convinced that I could successfully explore the literary world through this medium. After a few tries I assigned the Talking Books to a spot right beside the books Aunty Winnie and Granny had bought for me.

I found that there is a big difference between listening to the radio and listening to a Talking Book. With radio, the music is in the background, a part of the environment. When something catches my attention, I bring it to the foreground, and when the piece is finished, I push it back. *Similarly* with news and talk radio, I am not fully *conscious* of what is being said. I focus when an item catches my attention then defocus and let my mind go elsewhere. I listen in bites, not for long concentrated periods.

The Talking Book demanded a different type of listening. It required a more concentrated form, very distinct from the casual listening given to the radio. I found that the information from Talking Books was coming too slowly for me to give it my undivided attention. My mind would wander off, and when it came back, I realized that I had missed vital information. In a live situation, I heard what the *lecturer* was saying while my mind processed other related information. My mind would be kept interested and alert, my attention making little forays but always coming back to keep abreast with *what* was being said. With the Talking Book, my mind would just wander off. I have observed that normal readers are able to use Talking Books much more easily than I.

The Talking Books did not provide the help I had anticipated, so I reverted to my strategy that had brought me this far. I attended all my lectures, questioned my lecturers, discussed with my colleagues and relied on my memory. I had a *very* successful time at Ryerson. The extent of my success could be measured by the fact that I stood first in my graduation class, and I received the Don Hudson Award for creative ability.

CHAPTER 9
THE MASTER'S PROGRAMME

I ventured back into the workplace armed with my Ryerson Diploma in Radio and Television Arts. I found employment at York University in Toronto as a Television Producer in the Department of Instructional Aid Resources. However, I was not there very long before I kept hearing my mother's voice exhorting me to get the best education I could. With that in mind, two years later I was back at Sir George Williams University in Montreal pursuing the Television Option *of* a Master's Degree in Educational Technology.

I found the programme very demanding since at this level candidates were expected to undertake substantial amounts of the work on *their* own. I had a number of issues with which to contend. Reading was never and will never be my primary *source* of information. Libraries were unfriendly places, often conspiring to hide information from me. In the sea of books that was the library, I was like a rudderless vessel being tossed about with no hope of ever getting to the desired destination.

Just as a small rudder could be used to safely steer a craft, so too a little guidance was all that I needed to be able to make some useful incursion into the sea of stored information that was the library. While I would never read with the competence expected of someone with my ability and education, supervision and guidance would allow me to improve my performance.

An experience from my undergraduate years illustrated my difficulty with print. Professor Hector Massy, my Political Science lecturer, had handed me a book, which he said contained all the information I needed for the paper I was preparing. It was a fairly large book, and its size immediately made me anxious. He gave me no indication of the specific information the book contained. I was faced with a large amount of printed information in a small type font. I felt the nervous tension building as I stared at the tome. Later that night, I opened the book and turned the pages but I got no information from the words printed therein. I wondered why Professor Massy *had* given me the book, for it was as though he had handed me a book of blank pages. I could find no information that I needed. Had the print been large, I might not have been so intimidated. I have found large print to be much friendlier and easier to understand than small print. Large print with pictures would have been best. Maybe when it comes to print, my brain functions at a more *juvenile* level. A large book, small print and no direction rendered it very difficult for me to extract information from the printed text.

I returned the book three days later with my paper no further advanced.

"Did you get the information?" Professor Massy asked.

"No," I replied.

He was very *surprised*. He took a pad and proceeded to outline the information I should have gotten from the book. He tore out the page and handed it to me. Armed with this key I was able to unlock the book and the pages were no longer blank. They became full of information that I had been unable to discover before his assistance.

The *infinite* number of choices available in a college library immobilized me. I needed to be given specific direction in a structured environment. For the books to be of value I needed someone to find the section, the stack, the shelf and finally the book, and then I needed to be given some indication of what I could expect to find between its covers. *Fortune* smiled and gave me a bonus, sending me someone who was able to identify the *relevant* chapters in the books I needed.

The first day that I entered the programme I was pleasantly surprised to see that an old friend of mine from my first year at Sir George was also enrolled in the programme. We were carrying identical courses, and she was an avid reader. We teamed up and visited the library together. She located the necessary books and indicated the *relevant* chapters, thus making my reading task manageable.

I had successfully completed one of Canada's premier television production programmes and had had two years' experience in Educational Television at York University in Toronto. While she held sway in the library, the television studio was my domain, and here I could return the compliment.

We worked together and read each other's papers, which ensured that my misspellings were spotted and corrected. Reading no longer embarrassed me, as I simply refused to read anything without first preparing for it. Now that everything was in place, it was very easy for me to complete the course requirement. The thesis was the only impediment standing between the degree and me. Successful completion would make me the first member of my family to have entered university, received a university degree and a Master's Degree. But there would be a slip between the cup and the lip.

The Thesis Advisor assigned to me outlined what he considered an appropriate subject for my thesis. He was very enthusiastic. He thought that I should undertake a review of the publications released by the United Nations Educational, Scientific and Cultural Organization from 1945 to determine how their pronouncements on education in the developing nations matched what actually took place. He might have been enthusiastic, but I was not. Was I expected to locate and read UNESCO publications from 1945 to 1970? I needed help just locating and examining the content of a single book. How was I ever going to accomplish this task? I saw my Master's Degree slowly slipping out of my reach.

Just as I had gone to Rev. Walls and convinced him that my colleagues and I should be allowed to carry Biology in place of French, so too I approached the Head of the Education Department to argue my case for a new Thesis Advisor. I suggested to him that in an Educational Television Option there should be room for a thesis to be presented in that medium. Unlike the other members of the programme, I had entered with a strong television background and ought to be given the opportunity to present my thesis in that medium.

After consideration, it was agreed that if I were able to find an acceptable Thesis Advisor I would be permitted to submit a Thesis Equivalent consisting of a half-hour television programme accompanied by teaching material and a production script. I found a Thesis Advisor; Professor Douglas Burns Clarke, Professor of Fine Arts, who agreed to supervise my thesis equivalent. I produced the programme's first thesis equivalent, *From Ritual to Drama*. I successfully completed the requirement and I was awarded the Master of Arts Degree in the Spring of 1971.

I returned to York University and assumed the position of Media Coordinator in the Department of Instructional Aid Resources. I was in an academic *environment*, and although I was well accepted, I still found it necessary to hide the fact that I could not spell and did not read. I became aware that the Psychology Department was offering a speed-reading programme designed to vastly improve an individual's reading speed and comprehension skills.

A speed-reading programme was just what I was looking for, or so I thought. This one had an extra attraction. It came with a money-back guarantee. The cost of the programme was one hundred and twenty-five dollars. A participant who completed the programme with an attendance record of ninety percent or better would not only achieve an increase in reading speed and comprehension ability but would also get a full refund of the fee paid. Nothing could be easier or better. All I had to do was to attend every session and I would improve my reading skill at no cost.

I signed up, paid my money and took my chances as I showed up for my first class. The process was simple. The facilitator operated a tachistoscope, which was used to project text. At first single words were displayed for a reasonable *length* of time. But soon the words became phrases, and the display time was reduced to what I considered to be a flash. If I could not read a phrase at once when the words were fixed on a page where I could *stare* at them for as long as I wanted, how was I expected to read a phrase when it was flashed so fast that if I were to blink I would have missed it? It was most frustrating. I do not know which was worse, this or the typing course with Miss Gregg. Here I had the power to take action and I did. At the end of the third session, I told the facilitator that she was welcome to keep my money as I refused to allow myself to be subjected to that torture any longer. And just as Mummy, Miss Baxter, Miss James, Miss Meghu, Miss Gregg and so many others before, this facilitator was left to wonder why this *bright*, intelligent and articulate young man would experience so much difficulty performing the simple task of reading, this time the words projected by a tachistoscope.

My difficulty with reading and spelling did not hamper my progress at the university. Television was seen as the important innovation in the teaching and learning process. There was the University of Toronto, *Scarborough* College Television experiment, and at York University we had our professional television studio. I was involved with assisting the faculty members in developing and using television and other instructional media in the class- room.

I was in my office one day when Dr. John LaBaron visited me. He said that he came to me because I was highly *recommended*. He explained that since the Faculty of Education at York University was offering a pre-service concurrent *Bachelor* of Education degree, he was charged with offering a course that would *equip* students with the knowledge to be able to create and effectively utilize instructional media in the classroom.

I spent the better part of the summer working with John designing the course and assisting him by providing media *laboratory* support to the students enrolled in the summer *course* he was offering in the production and utilization of instructional media. The Faculty of Education had become my second home.

We finally designed the course. At my suggestion, it was being offered as two half courses: Non-print Media and the School *Curriculum*, and Film and Television in Education. I had done most of the design while John had written the rationale and proposal, which were presented to and accepted by the Faculty Council. Then, ten days before the start of the school term, I was summoned to the office of the Dean of the Faculty of Education, Professor Bob Overing.

Dean Overing was a tall, slim, very pleasant fellow, more like a brother than the Dean of the Faculty. "Fred," he said, getting right to the point. "You're aware that John has gone back to the States." I had run into John a few days before, and he had told me that he was off to the States and that he had recommended me as the best one to teach the courses, but I had dismissed his remarks. "John said you did most of the work in developing the courses. Everything is in place so we have to offer the courses. I'm asking you to teach them."

My blood ran cold. My mind was racing. Me teach a Media course to undergraduates? It was not that I lacked the knowledge or the *academic* credentials. I was active in designing the courses, but they were John's courses. I was only helping him. Yes, I was responsible for conducting media seminars for the Faculty. In those cases, I had all my material prepared. I demonstrated how they could effectively employ the various media and answered their questions. I was good at that. But teach? Did he know that I could not spell? Was he willing to have a university lecturer in the Faculty of Education who did not read and could not spell? I had an instant headache.

I became conscious of the Dean's voice as though he were far in the distance.

"And we will have you cross appointed to the Faculty as Course Director responsible for the two half courses. You will talk with Phil (Meredith). She will handle the necessary paperwork. So welcome to the Faculty," he said, and he extended his hand and we shook.

"Thanks," I replied as I left the room in a daze.

To the Dean it was a fait accompli. The Faculty would be offering the media courses and I would be teaching them. To me it was not that easy. If I accepted the offer, then I stood the chance of being *embarrassed* in front of the class because of my *inability* to spell. To refuse the offer, I would have to tell the Dean that I was doing so because I could not spell. Then the news would run through the campus like wildfire and everyone would want to see the fellow who refused a teaching appointment because he could not spell. I was caught between a rock and a hard place.

I returned to my office tortured by the decision I had to make. Two visions kept haunting my mind. In the first, I was standing in front of a class of undergraduates who were laughing and pointing to the blackboard, and I looked around embarrassed when I saw that I had written N-A-M instead of M-A-N. In the second, I was standing in *front* of the Dean, who was looking down at me and saying, "Let me hear that again. You're not accepting the teaching appointment because of what?" And with head bowed I replied hesitantly, "Because I can't spell, sir."

What should have been an easy decision was a tough one for me. The Dean had already decided that I was going to teach the courses. I had to accept or reject that decision and the less traumatic course of action was to accept. So I did.

I overcame my initial fear and successfully taught the two half courses, Non Print Media and the School *Curriculum* and Film and Television in Education. I enjoyed the experience and had a very good rapport with the students. My inability to spell and my difficult with reading were never an issue. The courses received very good student reviews. My association with the Faculty of Education and the courses ended when I decided to leave the university five years later.

CHAPTER 10

DRUM, TRUMPET, FLUTE, APPLE, SAXOPHONE

As a member of the Faculty of Education at York University, I was able to obtain a Minor Research Grant, which allowed me to produce a multi-image slide show designed to provide the teachers in training with a better understanding of the education system in Trinidad and Tobago. During my visit to Trinidad, I met Ms. Janet Baptiste-John who was offering a Special Education Programme in a classroom she had constructed under her house. I also met Dr. Esla Lynch who had established the Eshe's Learning Centre, a Special Education School. They both requested my participation in programmes they were organizing to highlight the needs of children who perceived the world similar to the way I did. They hoped that my presence and story would inspire the children and assure their parents that these children could lead successful and productive lives.

Dr. Lynch was a very interesting lady; she was also affected by dyslexia, a condition more commonly found in boys than girls. During her elementary school days she struggled as an *undiagnosed* dyslexic, and even suffered from the same severe dictation-spelling abdominal pains as I did. Her teachers thought that she was dumb and did not give her much chance for *academic* success. However, she proved them wrong as she obtained a terminal degree from the University of *Massachusetts*. After working as a Special Education Professional in the Toronto School District, she returned to Trinidad where she established a school to minister to the needs of special children.

Over the years Dr. Lynch invited me to participate in the in-service seminars she organized for teachers. For the closing event of one such seminar she invited three guest speakers: Father Jason Gordon, a Catholic priest who was a lecturer at the University of the West Indies, a successful businessman who was also a director of Republic Bank of Trinidad and Tobago and myself. We all had one thing in common—we were all dyslexics. The businessman, whose name I withhold because of his preference for *anonymity*, had a childhood experience similar to the one I had had with dictation and spelling. His fear of dictation and spelling manifested itself in the same physical ailment that had afflicted me: severe abdominal pains. His pains were so severe that his parents, who were very wealthy, took him to their family doctor who was convinced that his condition was life threatening. Acute appendicitis needing emergency surgery was the diagnosis. The surgeon who performed the operation removed a healthy appendix. This boy did not have a Mummy with a whip to cure him of the dictation and spelling induced abdominal pains.

When it was my *turn* to present, I stated that it was human nature to expect everyone to function the same way we do. The importance that society had placed on reading and spelling had given rise to some misconceptions. One of these was that everyone could acquire reading and spelling skills with competence. But there is no skill that every human being can acquire with competence, and reading and spelling were skills. With methods for coping and strategies for minimizing the negative effects, we were able to improve our performance and get better at handling situations that required reading, but some of us will never become competent at *reading* and spelling. This has nothing to do with intelligence or ability. It is just a consequence of being human.

In my talk that day, I strongly disagreed with the view that dyslexia was a reading problem, a learning problem and a learning disorder. Dyslexia was no more limited to being a reading problem than blindness was a reading problem. If dyslexia were a learning disorder, then I should have had problems learning. I never had any problem learning. I had difficulty with the method by which teaching was done. Educators who would readily admit that it would be idiotic to expect a deaf child to learn from lectures or a blind child to learn *from* reading printed books, saw nothing absurd when they expected me to learn from the written word.

What was spelling? To me, spelling was a number of objects placed in a row, and I was expected to recall all of the objects and the precise order in which they were arranged. What was reading? Groups of objects placed in rows that I was expected to look at, perceive their components in *their* original order and ascribe meaning to them. I was also expected to perceive the groups of objects and their components in the order in which they were originally presented.

I expressed the opinion that dyslexia, or word blindness as my mother called the manifestation, was merely a term, a label, a description as it were of how I perceived the world. It was not a condition that could be remedied or cured.

It was instructive to present some of the information that I had collected through the years *from* my experience with dyslexia. I suggested the following:

1. Dyslexics do not display identical symptoms.
2. When given verbal instructions to perform a series of tasks, they experienced difficult in recalling those tasks, especially in their proper order, and therefore in performing all of them.
3. Dyslexics may know all the objects in a series, for example the months of the year, but they experience difficulty recalling them in order.
4. Dyslexics have difficulty with spelling.
5. Dyslexics experience difficulty reading.
6. Dyslexics *experience* difficulty processing non-verbal cues and body language.
7. Dyslexics are unable to differentiate the sounds of the individual instruments of an orchestra or the phonemes that comprise words.

My challenges were compounded by my being forced to become right-handed. This resulted in my confused handedness. My hands have not given up their feud with each other for dominance. This fighting manifests itself in unexpected ways. A task as simple as reproducing the bossa nova beat is a challenge, as one hand first asserts dominance, then the other tries to take over, mixing up the beat.

I suggested that if objects were placed in a row I might *experience* the same difficulty calling them in order, since dyslexia was a *peculiarity* with perception and not a learning problem.

I *hypothesized* that if a dog, a yam, a sandwich, a lamp, an egg, a *xylophone*, an igloo and an apple were placed in a row and I were asked to name them, because of my history it was reasonable to assume that I might call some items in reverse order just as I did in reading and spelling. That rearrangement would not be considered significant nor would it change the meaning of the items in the same manner that my perceiving **w-a-s** as **s-a-w** did.

I held that because we dyslexics perceive our environment in this manner, we are often seen as being creative. We perceive our world as being fluid, where objects are free to move around and are not confined to a static order. Our brains are able to accept that we are free to reorder our environment and produce something new. Our peculiar way of perceiving the world becomes a serious handicap when we are asked to read, because we are not allowed to be creative with the printed word. Our inventive brains are required to perform the monotonous task of reproducing and giving meaning to the material in the precise order in which it was originally presented. Teachers have failed to appreciate our creative genius, which, if given free rein, would allow us to constantly create new words from the same mundane set of letters. Our brains actively *seize* every opportunity to turn things around and to perceive words and letters in a different order. Unfortunately, reading and spelling demand conformity, and do not cater to creative latitude. Our brains possess the ability to manipulate the mundane and to produce new and exciting creations, but when this creativeness is applied to words, it is discouraged and severely punished.

Because dyslexia is regarded as a learning disorder, children between the ages of eight and twelve are given remedial attention. By the teenage years, these individuals have acquired knowledge and information, developed coping strategies and invented ingenious methods for masking their difficulties that they are often thought to have gotten over *their* condition, when indeed they have not.

My teenage years were a very trying time for me. It was the period in my life when I first became aware of the opposite sex. I became very interested in girls, but I could not recognize signals coming from the girls who were interested in me. Girls were shouting:

"I care about you."

"You're special."

"Please notice me."

"I want to be your friend."

"I love you."

But all I heard was the deafening sound of silence, for the shouts were non-verbal, a language I did not understand. I went through periods when I could not understand why I could not find a girlfriend. I felt lonely and confused, for although I was popular , I did not know what I needed to do to attract a girl. I suggested that this was a serious problem, for in severe cases this feeling of abandonment and loneliness, of being unloved and unwanted, might lead to teenage *suicide*.

I fit into the dyslexic profile perfectly. I was a normal boy performing very well, but my world was drastically changed when I was presented with print. Were this an oral society my perceptual *peculiarities* probably would have gone unnoticed. While difficulty with reading and spelling was one of its *manifestations*, dyslexia was not a classroom *phenomenon* but an indication that my brain was processing information differently.

I was not only having difficulty with information I received through the eye, but also through the ear. My brain seemed incapable of differentiating subtle differences in sound. To employ an analogy, it seemed as though the filters in my brain were not fine enough, so while they were able to identify the dominant sounds, all others were heard as a single sound. My inability to identify the instruments in an orchestra was not very significant. However, spelling was almost impossible when I heard a short word or a syllable as a single sound and not a combination of *phonemes*. Ascribing symbols to unheard sounds was an impossible task.

I will never outgrow the way I perceive the world. The reading problems I experienced as a child are still with me today. I reverse and failed to perceive numbers, letters and words. Spelling remains a serious challenge. As my knowledge has increased and my understanding of the world has grown, I have become better able to identify many of my mistakes. I have also developed strategies to cope with and to mask my difficulties. I have developed excellent listening skills; I listen more and speak less. If I am faced with writing unfamiliar words, I search to see if I can find them written *anywhere* so that I can copy them correctly.

Reading has remained a challenge, and it is always a frustrating exercise. I still do not read for pleasure; in fact, I have not read a novel in over twenty years. I restrict my newspaper reading to headlines and opening paragraphs. I obtain most of my news and current affairs information through non-print media.

I explained how my performance continued to be baffling, since it was often thought that someone who butchered reading and spelling the way I did should not be able to write well. However, this did not hold true in my case, as my ability to write outshone my ability to read and spell. Although I do not read, I write much better than the average person. Even my brother Samuel, who is constantly reading, admits that he has difficulty with technical and creative writing and he cannot write as well as I can.

My experience has allowed me to understand how individuals who read profusely are often unable to write well. However, my writing ability has made it difficult for many to accept my inability to read and spell.

My distrust of the written word has resulted in an overwhelming reliance on the spoken word. When I am asked for directions, although signs might be clearly posted, I give non-literate cues, relying on visual and other markers.

One of the most important contributing factors to my success in navigating the Trinidad and Tobago elementary and *secondary* schools and the Canadian university systems without help from any Special Education teacher was the influence of my mother's strong belief in me. She believed that I could succeed, and she got me to share that belief. Mummy transformed that belief into action. She recognized that the Fred described by the teachers as lazy and careless was not the Fred she knew—industrious, careful, inventive, dependable and able to function effectively in the real world. She knew that something unidentified was responsible for my difficulty at school. She was willing to work with me to ensure my success.

Then I shared the story of Miss Baxter, my first teacher who was willing to take a chance with me. In a system, which did not cater to it, she recognized the need to structure my learning environment and individualized the instruction. She maintained control of my formal education until I had a solid foundation. I expressed my strong belief that the best teachers should be *assigned* to the entry classes, for a poor entry teacher would have made my father's *prophecy* come true.

At university, I attended well nigh all of my classes and interacted with my lecturers. I visited the library in the company of friends who *greatly* assisted me in locating *relevant* books. I relied *heavily* on my memory, making little use of notes and diaries.

My reading has not advanced beyond reading word by word, and if the word is long, I must read syllable by syllable, as I am unable to assimilate groups of words or phrases at a time.

Here are some examples of the way I misread text. The way the words originally appeared is presented first, and the way I read the words is written underneath:

Tarouba fiasco
Haunts T&T and Mr. Manning

I read: Trouble haunts T&T

Bob Nealy now
A Firebird

I read: Bob Nealy won a Firebird

Handpicked state chairman assists cops in…

I read: Handicapped state chairman…

3 PMs to meet on Caribbean Airlines

I read: 3 MPs…

Winston HARMS

I read: Winston Harris

82-4

I read: 84-2

When I was introduced to the game at age ten…

I read: When I was instructed to the game…

The years have passed and the children are now grown and live away from them…

I read: The years have past and the children live among them—"are now grown and" completely disappeared and "away from" became "among"

I have never been able to explain how I could have read:

Although my challenges had not disappeared…

as

All my children had not disappeared…

Many friendly conversations with people I have never met have resulted from the way I incorrectly dialled telephone numbers. Whether I was reading written numbers or instructing my fingers to dial from memory I somehow manage to get the numbers right but their order wrong.

After demonstrating to the seminar attendees the ease with which I can write backwards, I asked them to agree on a list of ten words with which they were all very familiar, as they were going to have a spelling test. When I was a child, my teachers routinely went through a spiel, never letting me forget how poorly I had performed on the previous spelling tests. They reminded me that I was given time to study the words; thus I was expected to be prepared. They exhorted me to do better and often threatened me if I did not.

I did the same to the group and then I said, "Dr. Lynch will call the words. Since I was considered very slow in class, her *pace* will be dictated by my performance. Oh, by the way, you saw how easily I did it, so you are expected to write the words backwards with the same ease."

A roar of laughter was the immediate response.

I asked why the laughter, and I pointed out that they were trying to let me know that the task was beyond them. I reminded them that in their classes, when little Johnny tried to convey a similar message, he was often deemed to be disruptive and unruly when all he was trying to say was, "Miss, I need help. That task is exceedingly difficult for me."

Then we began the test. By the time the third word was called, there were cries of, "Too fast!" and "Slow down!" and laughter emanated from the group. Dr.

Lynch merely disregarded their pleas. This generated louder and more urgent requests for her to slow down.

At the end of the exercise, not one of these bright, educated teachers had been able to complete what to me was a very simple exercise.

ILUSTRATION 3

Hold image in front of a mirror to read the words

During the discussion that followed, it was obvious that they recognized some important factors and that they had a better understanding of the plight of the dyslexic. One of the first things they recognized was that the normal speed for the average child was often too fast for the dyslexic child.

They also recognized that neither the ability to read and spell nor the *failure* to perform at the expected level were indicators of intelligence.

They better understood that:

- Effort did not always *bring* success
- Low achievement was not necessarily a result of laziness
- Mistakes are not necessarily a result of carelessness.

During the discussion, they spoke about the following:

- The frustration they felt
- How they could not keep up with the pace
- How they did not finish the exercise
- How they dropped out
- The anger they felt when their pleas for help were ignored
- Deciding that the task was beyond them
- Giving up and quitting

They also recognized how quickly they began to develop coping strategies during the test. One strategy used was to first write the word correctly, before writing it backwards while glancing at the correctly written word as a guide (something I never have to do). This emphasized the fact that not only was more time required to complete the exercise, but more importantly, that dyslexic children need to accumulate a body of knowledge before they are able to develop effective coping strategies. Knowledge provides clues when mistakes are made. Knowledge is a prerequisite for the development of coping strategies.

I reminded the participants that this was a simulation exercise, but dyslexic children, like the child I was, face an unsympathetic classroom and a hostile educational environment unless they are blessed with wise, caring, skilled teachers. I also reminded them that the problem does not merely show up when dyslexic children enter the classroom and *disappear* when they leave to go home. It affects all aspects of their everyday lives.

I discussed with them how one of the benefits of living in a human society is the collective use of the strength possessed by each individual. What each one does well contributes to the development of society. The person who is unable to draw or to play a sport or to dance is accepted as normal. We have accepted that normal people are unable to do some things well—that is, except when it comes to reading and spelling. The person who experiences difficulty with reading is often *labeled* as learning disabled. This is contrary to being human.

I reminded the participants that what I did **not** do well—read and spell— often overshadowed the many things I **did** well. Too often we dyslexics are *stigmatized* because of what we do poorly. Suddenly it was our fault for merely being human. Our personalities are then scarred because we cannot read. It is important that dyslexic children be assisted in improving their reading skills, but their *personality* and self-confidence should not have to suffer in the process.

I took the opportunity to stress that young *children* want to please and do not perform poorly in class because of carelessness or out of spite or bad-mindedness. There are always underlying reasons for poor performance. The parents who interact closely with their children on a daily basis gain important insights into their children's world and thereby glean pertinent information about any challenges their children are confronting. It is the responsibility of parents to take active roles in the education of their children and not abdicate this responsibility to 'experts'.

In summary, I reminded the participants that dyslexia was a condition that affects all aspects of the person's life. The difficulty with reading is only one manifestation of the condition called dyslexia. I was challenged to identify the sounds of the individual instruments in a band just as I had difficulty differentiating phonemes and ascribing the correct symbol to them, which had a negative effect on my spelling. I was unable to create mental pictures of words, so I have produced many incorrect spellings of the same word. The problems I had were not limited to reading and spelling but also affected my ability to effectively utilize non-verbal language. My brain was challenged to recognize and interpret symbols—graphic symbols as well as non-verbal symbols. I have experienced *difficulty* whenever I have been expected to read body language, facial expressions and books. This has had an adverse effect on my educational and social development. As a teenager, my inability with non-verbal language often left me lonely in a crowd. The shame and *ridicule* I encountered in my formative years negatively affected my personality. I was shy and hesitant to speak up in a group. I learned that I was the one who saw things wrong. I was unsure of myself and easily intimidated.

Finally, I invited the group to *participate* in a little game:

"Drum, trumpet, flute, apple, saxophone. Identify the one that *doesn't* belong," I asked.

They all shouted, "Apple!"

I told them of little Johnny who heard his classmate say, "Miss, Johnny so stupid he put down 'drum'."

The whole class laughed at him as the cold dark cloud of doubt, *embarrassment* and shame *descended* upon him, just as I had often experienced during my formative years.

Maybe he had a teacher like Miss Baxter, *because* she put her hand on his head and said, "Why, Johnny? Why drum?"

Looking up at her with eyes saddened by the humiliation he felt, Johnny replied, "Miss, a drum is the only one I don't put in my mouth."

They did not laugh anymore, for they realized that Johnny recognized a category that was not obvious to any of them. He had seen something that they had not.

"So you see," I told them, "We dyslexics, who my mother called word blind, are not stupid, or foolish, or lazy, or careless, or have ability that we simply choose not to use. We are normal human beings who just perceive the world a little differently. We dyslexics are different not disabled."

APPENDIX 1

The following is a simulation group exercise to allow the participants to gain a better understanding of what it is like to be dyslexic.

1. Decide on a list of ten words of varying lengths and syllables.
2. Get agreement from the group that they are all familiar with the words.
3. Provide writing material.
4. Announce that there will be a spelling test on these words, but they will be required to write the words backwards.
5. Select a control person whose . writing speed will determine the *pace* at which the words are called.
6. Do not alter the *pace* if the group requests it.
7. Afterward, conduct an open discussion on the exercise.

Some of the issues that will emerge include the following:

1. Disruptive behaviour
2. Pacing
3. Inability to cope with the demands of the assignment
4. Pleas for help being disregarded
5. Knowledge of the words is no *guarantee* of correct execution
6. Writing reversals
7. Developing coping skills
8. Frustration
9. Quitting
10. Appeal for assistance ignored
11. Lack of understanding
12. Incomplete assignments

The group should be reminded that this exercise is just a simulation, but the dyslexic child is faced with these challenges every day in the classroom and in the real world.

APPENDIX 2

GLOSSARY

[1]cosamahoe	local shrub
[2]C.M.	Canadian Mission
[3]turn fig	half ripened banana
[4]change me	assign a new passage
[5]rounders	ball game similar to baseball
[6]scotch	ball game
[7]locus	an uncommon fruit with the hard shell of a nut
[8]word blind	original description of dyslexia
[9]wotless	worthless
[10]E.C.	English Catholic
[11]fry-bake	bread made by frying small round pieces of dough
[12]cocoa tea	cocoa beverage
[13]fig leaf	banana leaf
[14]tinnin	galvanize
[15]pet	the soft inner portion of a loaf of bread
[16]Bemax	Trade name for a wheat germ preparation. A 30-g portion is a rich source of Vitamins B_1 and E, folate, copper, and zinc; a good source of iron; a source of protein, vitamins B_2, B_6, and niacin; provides 5 g of dietary fibre; contains 2.4 g of fat; supplies 120 kcal
[17]breaking beche	to skip school without permission
[18]steups	to suck one's teeth in disgust
[19]roast corn	barbecued corn
[20]fares	rendezvous with a prostitute
[21]buller	male homosexual
[22]make a tack back	return quietly
[23]ketch	catch

[24]benching	severe beating on the bottom
[25]bumsee	buttock, bottom
[26]tief	steal
[27]dotish	doltish
[28]buff	to insult, yell at or argue with
[29]Roy Joseph	Roy Joseph had a very distinguished career. At that time he was an elected member of the Legislative Council representing San Fernando and he was named the first Minister of Education of Trinidad and Tobago. Previously he was an elected Alderman on the San Fernando Borough Council and at one time he served as the Mayor of that Borough.
[30]watchekong	canvas sneakers
[31]liming	hanging out
[32]downs	tropical fruit
[33]went to town	wrote a great deal
[34]tottots	breasts
[35]Redifussion	speaker installed in a home to receive radio signals through a wired network
[36]lime	casual or informal social event
[37]fatigue	a group activity that targets one individual for verbal assaults in the form of jokes
[38]steupsing	sucking teeth as sign of disgust
[39]S.A.F.A	Southern Amateur Football Association
[40]S.A.F.L	Southern Amateur Football League
[41]TLL	Trinidad Leaseholds Limited
[42]primed up	taking some drinks in preparation for a night out

APPENDIX 3

MISSPELLINGS

A
abandoned	*abandaned*
academic	*accademic*
activities	*actitities*
achievement	*acheivement*
across	*accross*
adolescence	*adolesent*
afoul	*afowl*
agility	*ajility*
also	*laso*
amiss	*amis*
analogy	*analagy*
and	*adn*
anonymity	*annominity*
anxiety	*anziety*
anywhere	*naywhere*
appetite	*appitite*
Appendix	*Apendix*
appetizing	*appitising*
arguments	*argumenst*
assault	*asault*
assigned	*asigned*
assignments	*assigments*

B
Bachelor	*Batchelor*
barreling	*braelling*

because	*beacuse*
black	*dlack*
bring	*birng*
bright	*birght*

C

came	*acme*
ceiling	*cieling*
chronic	*cronic*
college	*colledge*
conducive	*condusive*
conscious	*concious*
consistent	*consistant*
continuing	*contuining*
correct	*corect*
course	*coures, cource*
creative	*cerative*
cruelly	*cruily*
curriculum	*cirrucumum, corriculum*

D

deaf	*deaft*
dealt	*delt*
descended	*decended*
deteriorate	*deterroriate*
dilapidated	*delapedated*
diagnose	*diagonose*
diagnosed	*diagonosed*
difference	*defference*
difficult	*difficulyt*
dilemma	*delimma, delima*
diminished	*deminished*
disappear	*dispear, disappear, dissapear*
disappeared	*dissapeared*
doesn't	*dosen't*

Appendix 3

dormitory	*domitory*
doltish	*dotish*
dresses	*dersses*
drummed	*drumed*

E
eke	*eak*
embarrassed	*embrassed*
embarrassment	*embarassment*
encounter	*incounter*
enrolled	*enroled*
environment	*envrionment*
equip	*equipt*
experience	*expereince*

F
failure	*failuere*
fantasy	*fantacy*
fear	*fiar*
fearful	*fareful*
fortune	*fourtune*
from	*form*
front	*fornt*

G
gallery	*galary*
genius	*genieus*
genuinely	*genuininly, genuingly*
girlfriend	*girlfrend*
goalie	*goalee*
graying	*greying*
greatly	*greately*
greedily	*greedely*
guaranteed	*guranted*

H
had	*adh*
heavily	*heavely*
her	*hre*
humiliating	*humilitating*
hypnotized	*hynotized*
hypothesized	*hypothecized*

I
impeding	*impeeding*
inability	*ianbility*
indicative	*indicitive*
ingenious	*ingenous*
innocently	*innosently*
insistence	*insistance*
intense	*intesne*
into	*inot*
intrigued	*intreagued*
infinite	*ifninite*
intervened	*interviende*
incense	*insense*
intercept	*interep*
is	*si*
it	*ti*

J
juvenile	*juvinile*

L
labelled	*labled*
laboratory	*laborotory*
leaven	*leven*
lecturer	*licturer*
length	*lenght*
lowly	*lowely*

M

manifestations	*manifistations*
manageable	*managible*
Massachusetts	*Massechettus*
masters	*mastres*
menial	*meanial*
misdemeanor	*misdemenour*
misspelling	*mispelling*
my	*ym*

N

naively	*niavely*
nonsense	*nonsence*
nostrils	*nostrels*

O

occasions	*occassions*
occurring	*occuring*
of	*fo*
old enough	*odl eonugh*
original	*orignal*

P

pace	*pase*
panic	*panci*
participate	*paritcipate*
peculiarities	*pecularities*
peculiarity	*pecularity*
pertinent	*pertenent*
performing	*peforming*
permanence	*perminance*
personality	*presonality*
pharmacist	*pharmasist*
phenomenon	*phenominon*
phoneme	*phonem*

phonemes	*phonems*
plain	*plian*
possess	*posess*
preparation	*prereration*
prescription	*perscription*
pursue	*persue*

R

reading	*erading*
regularly	*reguliarily, regulirily*
relevant	*revelant, relavent, relivant*
resilience	*resilence*
revelation	*revalation*
ridicule	*redicule*
risen	*resen*
road	*raod*

S

stare	I had problems with this word. I went from *steer* to *stear* then looked for *stair* in the dictionary before realizing that I needed 'stare'
Scarborough	*Scarbrough*
secondary	*secondayr*
sentence	*sentense*
semester	*semister*
seize	*sieze*
similarly	*similarily, similary*
spelling	*speling*
source	*sourse*
stigmatized	*sitgmstized*
stories	*Storeis, stores*
stubborn	*sutborn*
stupid	*studid*
suicide	*sucicide*
surprised	*supprised*

T

talk	*takl*
terrified	*terefied*
their	*thier*
term	*tearm*
torpedo	*torpido*
treacherous	*treterious*
turbulent	*turbulant*
turn	*tern*

U

ugly	*uguly*
unacceptable	*unaceptable*
undiagnosed	*undiagonized*
unsympathetic	*unsympathic*

V

vain	*vane*
very	*verry*
voice	*viose*
volatile	*volotile*

W

walk	*wakl*
was	*wsa*
watched	*watshed*
weight	*wieght*
welts	*whelts*
what	*hwat*
with	*iwth*
wrong	*worng*

X

xylophone	*xylephone*

Made in the USA
Charleston, SC
03 July 2012